Invocation of the Gods

About the Author

Ellen Cannon Reed, High Priestess of the Isian tradition, has been student and teacher of the Craft and Qabala for 16 years. She and her husband (and High Priest), Chris, have been active in the Southern California pagan community for the last eleven years. They live on a hill overlooking the San Fernando Valley. When she's not teaching and working with her coven, or writing, she enjoys embroidery, reading, and beadwork.

To Write to the Author

If you wish to contact the author or would like more information about this book, please write to the author in care of Llewellyn Worldwide and we will forward your request. Both the author and publisher appreciate hearing from you and learning of your enjoyment of this book and how it has helped you. Llewellyn Worldwide cannot guarantee that every letter written to the author can be answered, but all will be forwarded. Please write to:

Ellen Cannon Reed
c/o Llewellyn Worldwide
P.O. Box 64383-667, St. Paul, MN 55164-0383, U.S.A.

Please enclose a self-addressed, stamped envelope for reply, or $1.00 to cover costs.
If outside U.S.A., enclose international postal reply coupon.

Free Catalog from Llewellyn

For more than 90 years Llewellyn has brought its readers knowledge in the fields of metaphysics and human potential. Learn about the newest books in spiritual guidance, natural healing, astrology, occult philosophy and more. Enjoy book reviews, new age articles, a calendar of events, plus current advertised products and services. To get your free copy of the *New Times*, send your name and address to:

The Llewellyn New Times
P.O. Box 64383-667, St. Paul, MN 55164-0383, U.S.A.

Invocation of the Gods

Ancient Egyptian Magic for Today

Ellen Cannon Reed

1992
Distributed by:
W. FOULSHAM & CO. LTD.,
YEOVIL ROAD, SLOUGH, SL1 4JH ENGLAND

FIRST EDITION, 1992
First Printing, 1992

Cover painting by Randy Asplund-Faith
Interior drawings by Lisa Peschel
Interior paintings by Martin Cannon

Library of Congress Cataloging-in-Publication Data

Reed, Ellen Cannon, 1943–
   Invocation of the gods : ancient Egyptian magic for today /
by Ellen Cannon Reed.
    p.   cm.
   Includes bibliographical references and index.
   ISBN 0-87542-667-0
   1. Magic, Egyptian. I. Title. II. Series.
BF1591.R44   1991
133.4'3'0932—dc20   91-32383
                                                          CIP

Llewellyn Publications
A Division of Llewellyn Worldwide, Ltd.
P.O. Box 64383, St. Paul, MN 55164-0383

Dedication

To Ember and Qeshet, who taught me far more than I ever taught you. Without your work, I could not have written this book. I say it to you too seldom, so let this serve to tell you and the world how very proud I am of both of you.

And of course to Christopher, my Lord Bek, who is the wind beneath my wings.

Other Books by Ellen Cannon Reed

The Goddess and the Tree: The Witches Qabala, Book 1, 1989
  (Formerly *The Witches Qabala*, 1985)
The Witches Tarot Deck (with Martin Cannon)
The Witches Tarot: The Witches Qabala, Book 2, 1989

Acknowledgments

Thanks to Coven Ashesh Hekat and Coven Shadowed Moon for their participation and help.

My gratitude to William Bentley for creating the hieroglyphs used in this book. Michael Poe provided the information on wine.

CONTENTS

The Magic of Egypt 1

PART I   THE GODS OF EGYPT
    Personal Relationships with the Gods 7
    The Gods of Egypt 11
    Other Egyptian Gods 96

PART II   WORSHIP, RITUAL AND MEDITATION
    The Cairo Calendar 117
    Rituals 156
    Meditations 174
    Songs for the Gods 187

PART III   MAGICAL WORK—EGYPTIAN STYLE
    Magical Tools 208
    Hieroglyphs 227
    Divination 248
    Incenses and Oils 270
    Food and Drink 274

Glossary 278
Sources 284
Bibliography 289
Index 293

THE MAGIC OF EGYPT

The world's fascination with ancient Egypt is not new. Egypt intrigued the Greeks and the Romans. It has captivated archaeologists and still fascinates many ordinary people today, as well as those of us with "unordinary" interests.

My own interest in Egypt began at the same time I found my way home to the Craft, for the Lady I first called upon was Isis. She answered. That was 17 years ago, and my life has been Hers ever since.

Over the years, I've been more and more drawn to Egypt and its magic. I continue to try to learn what I can about it. But I'm a Witch, not an archaeologist, not a ceremonial magician. My interest is not only in magic, but in religion. In the Craft, magic (i.e., spell-casting) is secondary; service to the Gods is my first interest. My own religion colors and directs my life. Therefore, the majority of knowledge I've gained and will share with you comes through a *personal* knowledge of the Gods of ancient Egypt.

There are many books about the Egyptian Gods and about the magic of the land, but almost all of them are written by people who were writing about "other people's Gods." These authors wrote through the eyes of their own beliefs, as we all do.

For myself and others, however, the deities of ancient Egypt are *not* other people's Gods. They are *ours*. They are not abstract; they are not distant. They are personal, precisely because our work with Them has made them more real to us, a part of us.

Although their climate and culture were not like ours, the ancient Egyptians were not so different from Pagans of today. They, too, saw the Ultimate as God and Goddess, and saw the Lord and Lady in all that existed. They, too, perceived the majesty, strength and fertility in a horned animal (it happened to be a bull, not a stag, but still . . .). They, too, found lessons in the works of nature from which they learned of the Infinite from the Finite. They, too, had a

1

fascination with, and an understanding of symbols as a means of attaining of spiritual growth.

Because the Egyptians expressed so much in symbols, much remains despite all that which has been lost. They have left us the keys to some of their knowledge, and left ways to learn for ourselves, ways to learn and achieve spiritual growth. Our coven is working to discover the doors those keys open. What we have discovered so far is here.

Spiritual growth? She's said that twice now. What's all this spiritual stuff? I thought she was going to tell us about spell-casting the Egyptian way.

I never said that. I said I was going to tell you about the magic of Egypt. We often speak of two types of magic, referring to them as "high" and "low" magic. I'd rather use "spiritual" and "mundane" magic, since the terms "high" and "low" express a value judgment which I do not share.

"High magic" or "spiritual magic" is work done for spiritual advancement; "low magic" or "mundane magic" is done for physical or material gain. Both can be important. We are living in a physical, material world. Using magic to meet our material needs is just as appropriate, and as moral as using magic to achieve our spiritual needs. Magic is less than holy only if it is used for impure reasons.

In the Craft our approach to magic is through the Gods. Having done all we are capable of doing on this plane, we turn to magic, and will often ask the help, the guidance and blessing of individual deities. The Craft is first and foremost a religion. You might call magic a fringe benefit, a result of our beliefs.

Not all magical paths are Craft, and our attitudes toward the Gods can differ. For example, one of my students, a practitioner of ceremonial magic for a number of years, states that there is a difference between the attitude of ceremonial magicians and that of Witches. The ceremonial magician (unless, of course, he or she also happens to be a Witch) views the Gods as a type of energy to be manipulated. A Witch sees Them as beings to be revered, adored. Therefore, our magic would very definitely have religious overtones, would it not?

Magic can be done without spiritual aspects, so if all you are interested in is spell-casting, you might find some things of value here. (And you might learn some things you didn't expect.)

We are taught that the Gods are within us as well as without, that we are already a part of Them, equipped with Their powers. By learning of the Gods, we learn more of our own capabilities; We can't do all they can do (yet), we can do many things. The more we learn of Them, the more we learn of ourselves. The more we learn of ourselves, the more we learn of each other. The more we learn about each other, the more we learn about the Gods.

Although this book contains information on spell-casting, the magic of Egypt is more than ways to cast spells. It is the magic of growing closer to the Gods, the magic of learning the Mysteries of the Universe.

I do not pretend that the information in this book is exactly as it was taught in Egypt, but rather as those ideas might be taught now, in our culture. This has been, in a sense, an translation. When Edward Fitzgerald translated "The Rubiyat of Omar Khayam," he did not translate it word for word. He translated its spirit, without being confused by cultural differences. This is the kind of thing you will find here.*

For example, the ancient writings contain many spells for protection from scorpions. This is a good thing to know, but it would be silly to include such spells here since most parts of our country are not overrun with scorpions. But these same spells may be translated into powerful rituals for protection against other forms of negativity.

Much of this information, especially on the Gods, is the result of meditation and ritual work involving members of our coven. I've quoted them and mentioned them often. When you see the names Ember, Qeshet, Shava Shadar and Simara, consider yourself introduced to a member of the Coven of Sothistar.

Part I will show you the Gods as the members of Sothistar have learned to know Them.

Part II deals with festivals, rituals, meditation, music, and worship. In Part III, you'll find information on magical workings, spells, hieroglyphics, and divination.

A friend of mine who follows a Celtic tradition kept assuming that I would love Middle Eastern music, dress, etc., and for the

---

* In case you are among those who don't believe archaeologists can be mistaken, I refer you to a book called *Motel of the Mysteries*, by David MacCauley. It is fiction and humor, but it might make you think differently.

longest time I couldn't figure out why. Suddenly I realized that she made this assumption because she knew that I was interested in Egypt, modern Egypt is very different from ancient Egypt. It is Islamic, for one thing, and its people are Semitic—whereas those who lived in Egypt in the earlier dynastic times were Hamitic. To avoid any confusion between ancient and modern Egypt, I will use an ancient name for ancient Egypt—"Tamera," which meant "Beloved land"; and I will refer to its inhabitants as "Tamerans."

Travel to the past with me, to a land so important to its people that its name meant "Beloved land." Let me introduce you to it first through its Gods.

PART I

THE GODS OF EGYPT

PERSONAL RELATIONSHIPS
WITH THE GODS

Before we explore information on the individual Gods, I would like to discuss how I came by the information and the meaning of the title above. Exactly what do I mean by "personal relationships with the Gods"?

It is difficult to explain, but I'm stubborn, so I'll try.

One big difference between Wicca and many other religions is our attitude toward, and our approach to the Gods. To us, the Gods are not distant, unreachable, unknowable beings. Rather they are very close, knowable, reachable, touchable, lovable and personal.

In many covens, including mine, this attitude is put into practice by what is often called "Drawing Down the Moon." It is also called "aspecting" and "channeling." Though I avoid the latter term because of the meaning it has come to have in New Age usage. Basically it is this: The Priest calls the Goddess into the Priestess, who serves as the vessel. Ideally, the Goddess speaks through the Priestess. She may speak to the group as a whole, or to each member individually.

Imagine, if you have not experienced this, talking to the Goddess, holding Her Hand, asking Her questions, weeping on Her bosom (I have), professing your love for Her. (Of course, the same applies to an invocation of the God.)

Once this is experienced, your relationship with the Goddess or God is indeed on a more personal level than if your only contact with Her were kneeling before an altar. We are taught that the Gods are both within us and without, and a personal relationship with the Gods turns this statement from a concept to a reality—such a relationship makes Them real to us, more a recognized part of us.

You may be nodding your head with understanding. You know. You understand. Isn't it a wonderful feeling? Aren't they glorious to know in this way?

On the other hand, you may be frowning . . . not understanding.

If my explanation has not helped you to understand, it is no fault of yours, and not even mine. What I am trying to do is similar to describing what it is like to be in love. You must experience it for yourself. How? There are many ways, and every teacher has his or her own, but I can only tell you mine.

In this book, I will demonstrate techniques which were used in researching the Tameran Gods, techniques which may be used by you to build a relationship with any deity you choose. If you are a teacher, you can use them with your students, for the Gods you worship. If you are solitary, you can use them alone.

As I said earlier, I've never been content with the description of the Tameran Gods, Their attributions and qualities, as presented in most of the books available to us. I wanted to know who They *are*, how They relate to us *today*—not merely who Egyptologists think they were, and how they once related to the people of Tamera. So in addition to studying many books, I had to find other ways to learn about Them. Our coven set out to learn, and our first step was one that would and will shock some people.

We asked Them.

We began with two methods I'd been using for some time—mantra meditations and contact rituals, both simple techniques, with results that belie their simplicity.

The first is a form of individual meditation that can be done almost any time, any where. I have used it successfully walking from one place to another. (This does require a certain ability to have your mind in two places at once, but isn't all that difficult.)

You begin by breathing rhythmically: In-two-three-four, Out-two-three-four. (This is a great way to prepare for other types of meditation, too, or simply to relax.) Once the rhythm is established, you accompany the breathing with a mental chant of eight syllables:

O - SI - RIS - LORD - TEACH - ME - OF - THEE
IN - 2 - 3 - 4 - OUT - 2 - 3 - 4

Continue this mental chant, trying to mean the words, until something happens.

What could happen? I was chanting "O Lady Bast, teach me of thee," when I began to feel the tension that for me is a feeling of power, of energy gathering around me. I continued a moment more, until suddenly, inside my head (or was it?) I heard "SILENCE . . . " Believe me, I silenced, and as soon as I did, I heard ". . . is my name. In silence, shall I be heard." You'll find more of the results of that meditation in the section on Bast.

Once you have His or Her attention, once you feel that Presence, you can listen, feel, ask questions, whatever you like—in a respectful manner, of course. As soon as you can, make notes. Bast gave me a chant that has never failed to call Her. Other things have been learned from other meditations.

How do you know it isn't your imagination? You don't. If, however, you will work with the information received, such as the chant mentioned above, do further reflection and research, what is true will be proved.

The second approach to learning about the Gods was the use of contact rituals.* Although these are usually done by several people, they can as easily be done alone. These are very simple rites, almost group meditations, yet for all their simplicity, they have proven to be of immense value to more than one individual, to more than one group.

Detailed instructions for a contact ritual can be found in Part I. To do such a rite, we use the simplest circle casting possible, speak of the deity we wish to contact, ask Him or Her to be present to teach us about Him or Her self. If it feels right, we do a chant to the deity, sometimes a special chant, sometimes a free form one, and visualize the deity standing in the middle of the circle.

Although it is easier to have a picture, statue, or some other associated objects, to use as a form for visualization, we have quite successfully done rituals on a deity with only Her name. That was all we knew, and yet, it worked.

When the chant fades away, we are quiet, allowing each person to experience his or her own vision of the Lord or Lady. During the meditation, we may ask specific questions of the deity. Sometimes we just listen. It depends on the deity (with some, you just listen—you have very little choice).

Because these are private experiences, they are often very different from person to person; and yet, there is almost always an underlying thread of similarity. For example, when seven of us did a ritual

---

* Contact rituals were inspired by a type of ritual used by the Temple of the Elder Gods. Although contact rituals are very different, their seed was planted by a TOTEG circle.

to contact Tanent, a primeval earth Goddess about whom we knew absolutely nothing, five of us got the impression of one particular color—the same color in all cases.

We took the information gained in these rituals and worked with it. Ideas sometimes came to us later. (This is often true of meditations and rituals—the most important results do not occur during the ceremony.) We did other meditations on these Gods, and aspects on some. Those who were involved—students, friends, other covens—almost invariably gained something more than knowledge of the gods. They gained a relationship with them. To us, these gods are not abstract ideas or energies. They are not distant unreachable energies. To use they are known, and loved . . . greatly loved.

The third method of building relationships with the Gods is used by several teachers I know. This method uses guided meditations, pathworkings in which the student is introduced to the Gods in a guided visualization and then left to spend some time with Them. I have included several of these meditations in this book. Every one of these meditations is based on an experience with the deity involved, whether my own or someone else's. The words spoken by the Gods in these meditations were spoken in these experiences.

None of us will try to tell you that you will have exactly the same results with these methods that we did. Each of you is an individual, and the experience is intensely personal. If your view of the Gods is different, no matter. I would never try to impose my view of any God or Goddess upon someone else. I can only share with you what I have learned, and how. I do not insist that you see them as I do. I do not insist that you will develop the same intense love for and relationship with every deity you meet. However, I do believe that if you have not yet worked toward knowing any of the Gods personally, if there is not one God or Goddess you can say you know, you have some new joys in store.

I do promise you that if you use these techniques, and if you put yourself into them as we have, you will gain a treasure beyond price—a personal relationship with the Gods.

THE GODS OF EGYPT

Do you know Rhiannon, Cerridwen, Nuada, Kernnunos, Arian-rhod? Do you know Freya, Thor, Diana, Athena, Hecate?

Many people do. Many Craft people know and work with these deities on a regular basis.

Do you know Aset? Asar? Anpu? Het Heret? Nebet Het? If not, you might know Them by the names the Greeks used: Isis, Osiris, Anubis, Hathor, Nephthys. Some people know Their names, perhaps even a legend or two, but they do not have the close personal attachment to these Gods that they have to others. To many pagans, the Tameran Gods are too confusing, with their multiple names, animal heads, and ambiguous relationships. For many, the Gods of Tamera are unreal.

To me and the other members of Sothistar, however, They are very real—very personal, very much a part of us. We know many of Them, personally, and we adore Them. Each of us has a Goddess or a God we are closest to, who is, to use a feeble word, special to us—perhaps more than one.

Many Craft groups concentrate on one pantheon, the Gods of one culture, and for those groups all aspects of the Lord and Lady can be found in the Celtic, the Nordic, or Greco-Roman.

Although I truly fit in the second category, for I have a special love for Odin, the Morrigan, and others who are not Egyptian, in this book my main concentration is on the Egyptian.

Why? Certainly not in hopes that all who read this book will switch from the deities they work with to the Egyptian, but in hopes that you may find one or more deities here who can join the company of those for whom you have a special affection. Generally, I hope to give an understanding of "my" Gods to those who have not yet met Them.

This book is not an attempt to recreate the worship of these Gods as it took place all those centuries ago. We are not ancient Egyptians—our culture, our climate, our very mindsets are different. One might think that these differences would preclude any relationship with their Gods—but, oh, my friends, not so! (We are not ancient Celts, either, whatever our blood lines.)

Most of these Gods do not fit neatly into the traditional archetypes of Maiden, Mother, Crone, or Sun god, Earth god, etc. Again, one might think that would preclude using them in a Craft group, and again, oh, my friends, not so!

It is possible that what you find here may satisfy a greater need. The Craft is an experiential religion, and in order to provide the most effective experience, all facets of its practice must resonate for the practitioner. Although most who follow this path work with the Celtic Gods and find themselves fulfilled, there are those who are drawn to this religion who find that the Celtic Gods do not touch their hearts in the way necessary to experience this fulfillment. Perhaps it is to these people that the Egyptian Gods might sing.

Because so many of his books have been made easily available, E. A. Wallis Budge is, to the average person, probably the best known expert on the subject of ancient Egypt, its people, its religion. What many of you know of these subjects may well have come from him. You may have discovered other authors. A glance at the bibliography of this book will give you even more sources for information.

As mentioned earlier, only part of what is found here is taken from those references. Even if you've read widely on the subject, you might be in for a few surprises. If you've come to know these Gods and Goddesses personally, you might recognize many an old friend.

You will note that the names by which I refer to these deities may not be the names by which you know Them. There's a very good reason for that. In this book, and in most of the work we do, we use Their Tameran names, not the better known Greek versions of those names. It has long been a source of irritation to me that those Greek names are the most used, even in books on Egyptian history and Egyptian religion. I find it disrespectful.

The problem does not lie only with archaeologists and historians. Sometime ago I was talking with someone who was drawn to a particular Egyptian Goddess. I pointed out that the name Hat Hor (not Hathor) was the Lady's name in Greek. Her name in Tameran was

Het Heru or Het Heret. "I don't think so," was the response. "I think Hathor is Her Name, and the others are just titles." Oh, please!

In a recent special about the Great Pyramid, the Pharaoh who built it was constantly referred to as Cheops. At one point, the moderator pointed out some hieroglyphs that spelled "Khufu," and told us that was Egyptian for Cheops. No! "Cheops" is Greek for Khufu!

Whether They are new to you or not, come. Let me introduce you to these deities so very dear to my heart.

ASET (Isis)*

Seek you magic with wings?

I begin with the Lady who is probably the best known of the Tameran deities. She is also the most difficult for me to write about.

"What?" you say. "Everyone knows about Aset. How can it be hard to write about Her?"

It's hard because She is my Lady. I am Her Priestess. I have dedicated all my life to Her and the work she wants me to do. She came in to my life and brought with Her purpose, direction, and meaning. You'd think that would make it easy to write about her, but it doesn't. No words I can find will do Her justice, no dictionary or Thesaurus contains them. I will never feel I have succeeded in showing you Her Beauty, Her Magnificence, Her Power, Her Splendor, Her Love.

---

*The names in parentheses are the names by which these deities were known to the Greeks.

14

Who is She? Mother, Worker of Magic, Creatrix, Queen, Sister. She usually portrayed in one of three forms; wearing the Solar Crown, or the throne that is her name, or her winged form. In Egypt, She was the epitome of loyal wife, mother, and ruler.

Don't let the term "loyal wife" confuse you. We are not talking about the "little woman," or the woman behind the man who has no place of her own. Aset's status was and is equal to that of Asars. When He traveled to teach the rest of the world, Aset ruled Egypt.

In our tradition, the Lord and Lady are given equal honor. Both Aset and Asar ruled Tamera. Both are the height and heart of our coven.

In ancient times, those who had lost a loved one would appeal to Aset for comfort, for She knew their pain. Those who had suffered because of love reached out to Her, for She understood. She defended Her Son against everything from scorpions to Set. Parents appealed to Her for protection for their children.

Those of any age who felt the need of a nurturing Mother turned to Her. I know. I have, and She held me.

She performed the greatest act of magic—She gave new life to her murdered husband, at the same time conceiving their son, Heru. There are many paintings of Aset hovering over her love's body, fanning the breath of life into Him with the wings of a bird.

Some writers call this bird a swallow, some a kite. I suggest another possibility, the African swallow-tailed kite, a relative of the hawk. Like the hawk and the vulture, the kite is a raptor, possessed of talons that grab and hold. I can hear you now, "Sweet lovely Aset, symbolized by a predator? How can you?" I can, and do.

Let me remind you that *we* are the animal kingdom's most voracious predators, and that all life feeds off other life. The bird of prey hunts down its food and kills it. So does a swallow, although its prey is usually an insect, so to some that makes it all right. An insect, even one we don't like, is still live prey. This attribution of a kite to Aset is appropriate because the kite gives a feeling a strength that is not found in a swallow. Aset is no Southern Belle who gets the vapors when things become difficult, but rather She is the epitome of woman, strong and powerful as well as beautiful.

Her name, Aset, means "throne," one of the symbols of a ruler. Without a throne, a king is not a king, nor a queen a queen. Without a throne, a seat, we stand alone on our two fragile feet. In a chair, we are stable, supported, steady, held. It is Aset who can hold us, make kings and queens of us, lift us heavenward.

The crown She often wears is called a "solar crown," or "horned crown." (You'll see Het Heret wearing it, too. Aset usually has the vulture headdress on as well.) The curved horns represent not only the cow—a Mother symbol to the Egyptians—but also the horns of the waxing and waning moon. The disk between, called the "solar disk," does represent a Sun, but not our Sun. It represents Sirius, the home of Aset, known as Sopdet to the Egyptians, and Sothis to the Greeks. Sirius is called "the Sun behind the Sun," the source of its power. It is to our Sun, some say, as our Sun is to our Moon.

Sirius is the brightest star in the sky and is easy to find most of the year. Locate the constellation Orion, usually identified by the three stars that make up his belt. You'll notice the third star to Orion's right is just a little off line from the other two.

Start with the star farthest to your right (his left) and draw a line through the middle star. As you continue past (not through) the third star, you will find Sirius. It is the brightest star in the heavens. If there is something brighter up there it is a planet or possibly a satellite. Legend says that sirius was the original home of Aset. Another legend days that Aset and Asar went to Sirius after they left Earth. Sirius is a double star. There's a subject for meditation for you!

Sothistar is, of course, named in honor of that bright Sun. It is our inspiration, a physical symbol of our goal in life. We seek to be bright and shining for Her sake, in Her Honor, and to Her Glory. For us, it is as much as symbol of the Goddess as is the Moon.

I use two stones for Aset. The first is azurite. It was a very precious stone in Egypt, its use restricted to priests. The finest pieces look like blue banded malachite. As a matter of fact, azurite and malachite are often found together in nature.

Another stone is chrysocolla, a beautiful stone of blue and green. Both of these attributions are the result of meditation. In contact rituals or other meditations, we often ask the God or Goddess we are communing with if there are special stones (or incenses, or chants, etc.) we should use as His or Her symbol.

How do you use a stone for a God or Goddess? We often give such a stone to someone as a symbol of that deity. If a special work is done that applies to a particular deity, the right stone, charged for that purpose, would be that much more effective.

The Romans fell in love with Aset, and took Her worship home with them, spreading Her fame even farther. A temple of Aset has been found in England. Statues of Aset nursing Her Son, Heru, may well have inspired the many pictures of the Madonna and child that came later. One problem we found in working with the Tameran Gods was the lack of a sea Deity. The Romans, however, saw Aset as a Sea Goddess, and held an annual ceremony in which their ships were blessed by the Goddess. Not everyone saw Herin Egyptian style or dress. A beautiful description of Her in nontraditional attire can be found in Apeleius' *The Golden Ass*.

Many people then (and now) saw Her as I do, the Goddess, the Lady in whom I find Nebet Het, Bast, Het Heret, Morrigan, Rhiannon, Freya, and all the other Ladies upon whom we have called over the centuries. When we call upon Her in Sothistar's rituals, we are calling all the Goddesses, all the many aspects humankind has given form to, all the names by which the Lady has been called over the centuries.

Although *I* will probably never feel any of my words will ever do Her justice, I have found the words of another that *are* worthy of Her.

Isis

"She lives in the endless murmuring of the sea or streams; gleams and sparkles in the sheen of stones; laughs or whispers in the rustlings of leaves and dwells in the glow of Sunlit things or the soft, silent shadows of the night. She is night and her children are the stars. She is Twilight . . . the Opening Between Worlds . . . and quiet becomings and growth in the secret recesses of the Earth. She lives in love, laughter, wonderment and delight in women and men and can be found in anything that helps bring one to see Her realm and sway . . . existence . . . as a 'beautiful festival of heaven and earth.' She dwells in the sky as the silver sheen of the Four-Fold Moon and its pale quiet light; She is the spiny coolness of the air and the refreshing caresses of soft winds. She is the stark, gaunt majesty of the mountains and the green softness of hills; She dwells in the wellsprings of the self where one goes to draw nourishment and strength for one's being. She lives in the sustaining and nourishing qualities of what one drinks, eats, or breathes, offering and giving of Herself to preserve one alive; She is the sustainer of souls and the spirit of quiet, relentless sureness of self; She is the Mistress of Mysteries and a lamp in the darkness to all who would seek Her and learn of Her ways. She can be as cold as ice and yet burn like fire as She seeks to help bring all to wholeness, completion, and transfiguration. She is the Womb of time and Being and all dwells in and as part of Her."

Formally, She is the August Dweller at the Threshold, Mistress of the Luminous Darkness, Mistress of the Fields of Heaven, Lady of Words of Power, Swift Huntress of the Soul, Throne of Being, the Splendid Light Who Veilest in Brilliancy, Dweller in Stillness, Lady Who Opens the Year, Lady of Abundance, Lady of the Fields, Lady of the West, Lady of the Mysterious Peace, Creatrix of Green Things, Queen of the Great House, Lady of Wild Things, Lady of the Dawn, Mother of the Golden Heru who Answered for His Father, Wife of Asar Millions of Years, Healer of Broken Dreams, Protector of Anpu, Lady of Silver, Lady of the Endless Quiet Light, Opener of Life, Lady of Silence, Beloved in All Lands, Divine One, Only One, Greatest of the Goddesses and Gods, Greatest of the Dwellers in Nun, Female Ra, Female Horus, Eye of Ra, Lady of the New Year, Maker of Sunrise, Lady of Heaven, Light-giver of Heaven, Lady of the North Wind; Queen of Earth, Most Mighty One, Queen of the North and South, Lady of Warmth and Fire, Benefactor of the Other World, Lady of Life, Lady of the Green Crops, Lady of Bread, Lady of Beer, Lady of Joy and Gladness, Lady of Love, Maker of Kings, Daughter of Geb, Daughter of Neb-er-Tcher, Child of Nut, Wife of the Lord of Inundation, Giver of Life, Goddess of Fields and Lands, Goddess of the Harvest, Mistress of Silence, Great Lady of the Other Worlds, Hidden Goddess, The Power of the Nile, Fertility Through Waters, Goddess of the Gods' Food, Transformer of Bodies into Bodies of Light, and Producer and Giver of Life.

She dwells in the depths and heights of every being. If you call to and from them, She will answer you. If you prepare a place within your heart for Her to dwell, She will be living within you. So will all the other Goddess and Gods.

First printed in *Khephera* 1975

Ron Myron

Isis and Osiris

ASAR (Osiris)

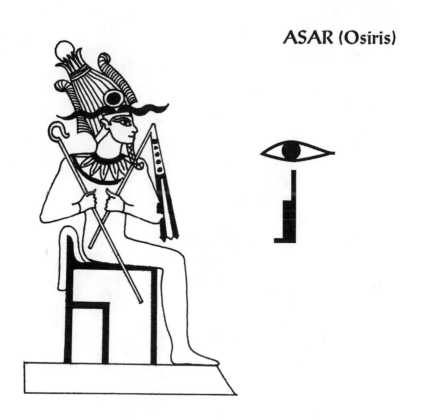

Pharaoh of two lands,
Hold us in your hands,
Osiris, Lord.

Except for Aset, Asar is probably the most widely known of the Egyptian Gods. He is also one of the least understood, for only one of His Aspects is known by most people.

We know Asar as the Lord of the Underworld, as the Judge, because most of our information comes from tombs. Such writings are, of course, very much concerned with death and the afterlife, and would tend therefore to emphasize this aspect.

Asar, the Judge, presided over the Weighing of the Heart, during which the heart of the deceased was weighed against the Feather of Maat, She Whose Name is Truth. If the result was favorable, i.e., the heart was as light as the Feather, the deceased went to live in the Fields of Ra; if not, the deceased was turned over to Amit, the Eater of Hearts.

These ideas portrayed on the wall paintings found in tombs differ from my own beliefs. I believe that should the deceased fail the test, it simply meant the soul had more work to do, and would return to Earth for another incarnation. This is just one way in which Sothistar's practices differ from the ancient traditions.

Asar is usually depicted in mummy wrappings, wearing what is known as the Atef crown. This is similar to the White Crown of Upper Egypt, with the addition of a feather along both sides, and a small sphere at the top. He holds the crook and flail, symbols of rulership.

In some paintings, His skin is black. In Egyptian symbolism, this color represented the Underworld and Rebirth. In others, His skin is shown as green because He was also the Lord of Vegetation. This aspect of the Lord is seldom mentioned, but one which I cherish.

As God of Vegetation, Asar would, of course, represent the Life, Death and Rebirth cycles of the grain and other plant life. Asar, Judge, Lord of Death, is concerned with the dead, but remember, the dead are also those who will be reborn. Thus in both aspects, Asar is the Lord of Life. This aspect I hold dear is Asar, the King.

I've found only one picture of Asar without the mummy wrappings. Even then, the picture did not even hint at the power of the God I have met in my meditations.

I have seen Him, strong and bronze, solidly built. His Face manages to be both beautiful and powerful. In my vision, He wore a nemyss and short kilt of blue and gold stripes, and a pectoral of lapis lazuli.

His presence was so overpowering that I fell to my knees, overcome, not by fear, but by awe. He was vital, vibrant, and inspired a devotion I was never able to give to His other aspect, however much I revered Him. This is the Asar adored and worshipped by our coven. This is our High Lord.

There is nothing of the solemn judge in this aspect, but that is not to say He is frivolous. He is not all sweetness and light. He is, after all, a king, and rules his people in a way that is best for them, guiding and protecting them, and punishing wrong-doers.

This is the meaning of the crook and flail with which is He is always portrayed. The crook is a shepherd's crook, symbolizing leadership. The flail symbolizes His duty to punish those who do wrong. No ruler is worthy of the title unless he or she is willing to do both. Balance is the keystone of many religions, including our own.

These symbols can be held by either aspect of the Lord, and the differences they might have when held by one or the other are worthy of contemplation.

Take a moment, if you will, to consider what these symbols would mean if held by Asar, the King.

Now think what meanings they might have when held by the Judge. Do you find differences? If so, what are they?

Life and death . . . both are important, both are part of the cycle we recognize. Asar's death and rebirth are celebrated time and time again in Tameran writings. Yet, death and resurrection mean nothing if not preceded (and followed) by life.

One of the most delightful customs recognizing His function as Vegetation God was known as an "Asar bed" or a "corn mummy." (Because corn as we known it in the United States is native to the Western Hemisphere, "corn" probably meant "barleycorn.") This is a shallow container in the shape of Asar, filled with soil and planted with grain. Many have been found in tombs. At the proper season, the corn mummy would be watered. The grain would sprout and the God would reborn.

If such containers were available today, I would plant them in the Fall. It is as this time of year that the Goddess does Her planting; fruits fall from the trees, grain from the stalk. Planting an Asar bed would be a wonderful thing to do during an Autumn rite. I would water it at Yule.

Asar is said to come from a star referred to as Orion. Older astronomy books identify this as the middle star on the belt of that constellation. It is green. Betelgeuse, the star at Orion's shoulder, was attributed to Set because it is red.

Partly because of the pectoral Asar wore in my vision, I use lapis lazuli for Asar. I have a lovely piece on the altar near his statue. This attribution comes not only from a meditation on Asar, but also one on Aset, when two of us were told that lapis belonged to Her Lord.

There was a barley field through which the Lord and I walked in my meditation, and where He spoke to me. Barley was grown in Egypt, and used to make both bread and beer. After some research and experimentation, we've developed a recipe for barley beer which we have used for celebrations honoring Asar. It isn't necessary to make your own. Malt liquor would serve as well. "Malt" is any grain (often barley) steeped, sprouted and smoked, so malt liquor is very likely similar to "barley beer."

Another symbol of the Lord was a pillar called the "tet," often called "Asar's backbone." It has the same sound as another Egyptian word meaning "stability." This, too, could be a part of the meaning of the symbol. No one seems to be certain. To me, it represents the stability and strength of the Lord. If it is, as some believe, the trunk of a tree, then the tree is a mighty one—a tree that withstands storms, earthquakes, the extremes of the seasons. Many trees, even if cut down, will grow anew from the stump left behind. Life arising from death—wonderful symbol of resurrection!

Although His Name is Asar, the hieroglyphs which spell his name say something else. The first symbol is an eye, "ari"; the second, a throne, "ast," or "aset." "Throne maker," or "made by the throne?" I don't know, but again, I'm sure we can learn much from contemplation.

I am not forgetting Asar's other aspect, the Lord of Death and Resurrection, nor is He any less beloved of our coven. I believe the best way to tell you about him is to describe the events that helped us know and love Him.

In class one night, we were discussing psychic gifts. After sitting quietly, her thoughts apparently turned inward, Shava Shadar burst out "I have a talent that is a curse! I help people through the veil. When I was little, I thought I was making them die."

"A curse?" I cried. "Oh, no, never!" We gathered around her, reminding her that making it easier for someone to leave this life was far from a curse. It meant that instead of leaving one's body in fear, one left holding her hand, led to the Summerland by her bright loving spirit.

A visitor in the class that night, has done similar work many times—she's a nurse—and she added her assurances to ours.

Shava Shadar's expression showed her thoughts were moving quickly, but she was still not assured until I said, "You take them to Asar. This is the work done by His Priests."

She has one of those faces which are beautiful in repose, but shining when she smiles. That glorious smile of hers said it all. She already loved Asar, the King, with all her heart. How could it be anything but joyful to take someone to His Presence!

She began to learn more of Asar, Lord of the Underworld, bringing to that study the love she already had for His Aspect as King. And as she extended that love to His other aspect, so did the rest of us. You should hear her say His name.

A short while ago, we were asked to do a healing for a lady. Barbara, a beloved friend of two of our members, was horribly ill with cancer.

Such work is always preceded by meditation. For that reason, I knew, when we opened that circle that we had to do more than physical healing. Healing was needed not only on more than the physical plane, but also was needed to extend to more than Barbara. We also had to heal Qeshet and Ember, who loved her so much. We would do our best to heal the cancer, but it would have been dishonest to ignore the possibility that it was time for her to go.

We did raise the healing energy, and gave it to Barbara to use as she willed. We reminded all present that those who cross over go to the arms of the Lord and Lady. We gave her three stones and suggested that, whenever her time came, she try to have these near her. The first was an apache tear, for Anpu, the Guide. The second was a lapis lazuli for Asar. The third was an azurite/malachite for the Lady.

Each of us took a little of her pain, and gave back peace and healing.

I then called Shava Shadar forth, and put her hand in Barbara's, telling Barbara to remember the feeling of her hand and to look for Shava Shadar's beautiful face when the time came.

We continued with our regular ritual, and by the end of it we were all laughing, including Barbara.

Two weeks later, Barbara crossed over, and Shava Shadar led her.

Did our healing rite fail? I think not. Her last two weeks of life were of higher quality than they might have been otherwise, needing less medication and getting better sleep. And she left a pain-wracked body without fear, led by a loving hand, accompanied by our beautiful sister, Priestess of Asar.

If you can understand and accept the above, you can accept and love the Lord of the Underworld. The important thing to remember is that the Lord of Death is still the Lord of Life, one who has experienced death and rebirth. When we die, He greets us, shows us what we have learned and have yet to learn, and gives us again to the Goddess who gives us birth once more.

Loving the Lord of Life makes it not only easy, but necessary to love the Lord of Death, for the dead are also the unborn!

King of Life and Death
Fill us with your breath
Osiris, Lord

I am the darkness of the womb
I am thoughtful silence

This Lady appears in many wall paintings and is mentioned in many writings, yet little is known about Her. She is the sister of Aset and Asar, wife to Set, Mother of Anpu. Her name means, "Lady of the House." She assisted Aset in the magical work done to resurrect Asar.

All this does not tell us who She is. When I determined to learn more, I was constantly frustrated. Book after book said little more than I've already written. So, I followed my own advice and used one of the methods I have described earlier. I chanted, "Oh, Nebet Het, teach me of Thee." This was the answer.

"Child, if you would seek me, seek me not. I am that which is not what it seems to be. By misdirection do I teach. I am the unseen."

Work with Her since has shown me who She is, at least as much as I can understand. Her energy seemed familiar to me, yet was different.

She is the dark side of the Moon: It is there, it is part of the whole, it is an integral part of the Moon, and we never see it.

Who is She? She is Aset. She is not a separate Goddess, but the lesser known side of Aset. Aset is the Silver Moon; Nebet Het is the dark side of the Moon. Aset is magic; Nebet Het is mystery. Lecturing is an Aset form of teaching. Guided meditations are Nebet Het style.

How can we learn more about Her? I don't know. I don't think you can reach for Her. She must come to you. I think She comes more often than we know. I think most of the things we learn indirectly are from Her.

In the movie *Karate Kid*, the young hero is taking karate lessons from an older man. He is given work washing and waxing cars, varnishing fences, sanding a floor and painting a house. Each job had to be done with very specific movements.

When the boy finally objects, his teacher shows him that in the course of performing the chores, certain movements became second nature, movements that are part of the martial arts.

That's Nebet Het. When we suddenly realize that something we've learned has proved useful in a totally unexpected way, that's Nebet Het.

Her presence in a ritual can be confusing because it's so like that of Aset, and yet so different. (Some call her the Dark Aset.) I had a phone call the other day from a High Priestess of another coven who asked if we worked with this Lady. Upon my answering positively (or "positively!"), she described an aspect they'd experienced in a Moon rite recently. The Lady had been indirect, independent, and the results of Her words and actions turned out to be very different from what was expected. "That's Her!" I said.

Although Asar and Aset are High Lord and High Lady of Sothistar, and those who reach Second Degree will be Their High Priest or High Priestess, members of Sothistar may also make special dedications at First or thereafter. Choosing (or being chosen by) a deity to dedicate yourself to can be a joyful experience, like being in love.

With the approach of her First Degree initiation, Simara was still unsure who she'd make a dedication to, if anyone. She was drawn to Aset, but felt in her heart that it wasn't quite right. She didn't know.

We did an aspect of Nebet Het in which I served as a vessel. As I/She stood in front of Simera, I found myself unable to speak the thoughts that were coming to me. The thoughts were very clear— Nebet Het was claiming Simara as Her Priestess—but I just could not get the words out of my mouth.

After the ritual, we discussed the aspect and when Simara spoke, I learned that it hadn't been necessary for me to speak. She and the Goddess had been having a conversation as I stood there—and she now knew she would be a Priestess of Nebet Het.

You can call upon Nebet Het if you wish something to be hidden, especially if you cannot hide it anywhere. You can call upon Her to help you teach in Her Manner. Am I being obscure? It isn't deliberate, I assure you. It's the Nature of this Lady.

Because I am dedicated to Aset, I am dedicated to Nebet Het also. I am spending, and will continue to spend, a great deal of time learning about this aspect of my Lady. The more I learn of Her, the more I love Her. And, as you known, loving the Lady in Her many aspects is always a joy.

Nephthys, Nebet Net
Dark Lady of Mystery!

Sekhmet and Bast

Cat with eyes of golden flame
Mau Bast

It is possible for you to skip this chapter and learn of Bast all by yourself. You can do it by using a chant I received from Her in meditation. It's very simple, only two words. MAU BAST. (Mau is the Tameran word for "cat.")

The words are chanted in a monotone, with the sound of each letter drawn out as much as possible:

MMMMMMMMMAAAAAAAAAUUUUUUUUUUBBB-BAAAAAASSSSSSSSST

My coven has used this on several occasions and it has never failed to result in Her Presence, in cat form . . . about 18 feet tall.

I spoke earlier of a mantra meditation I did on Bast, and promised I would give further details. As I told you, I was chanting "O Lady Bast, teach me of Thee," when I heard in my head "SILENCE . . . " I stopped my mental chant and tried hard not even to think. I heard " . . . is my name. In silence shall I be heard."

For a time, I simply noted the feel of Her presence. That feeling was very probably not what you would have expected, for Bast is not a cuddly kitten or an affectionate house cat. She is a Dark Lady.

In the Craft, Dark Ladies are usually referred to as Crones, or Hags. Often, they are portrayed as old women, but Crones, Dark Ladies, are not necessarily old. In our hallway we have a glorious picture of Hecate in which the Lady is pictures as young and voluptuous—and every inch a Dark Lady.

They are found in many traditions, in many pantheons. Among the best known are Hecate, the Morrigan, and Kali. If I say that I love and adore these Ladies with all my heart, what is your reaction?

Are you horrified? Are you frightened? If I started to invoke Hecate, would you run from the room? Do you think they are evil, mean and nasty?

If you do feel that way, you are certainly not alone; but if you continue to feel that way, you'll never learn much.

Those who refuse to deal with the Dark Ladies (and Dark Lords) are usually those who feel that any event that is difficult or painful is bad, is evil

Where is it written that all your lessons are easy ones? The important ones never are! Never!

Problems which are easily solved are easy because you already have the knowledge to solve them. Hard lessons require learning—that's what makes them hard!

The hardest of these lessons come from Dark Ladies and Dark Lords. Mother Goddesses will teach you table manners. They will hold you and comfort you, and when you make a mistake they will stroke your hair and say, "My darling, perhaps you should consider that you might have handled the situation another way."

Dark Ladies will hit you on the head with a 2 by 4 (just to get your attention) and say, "Hey! You screwed up! Fix it!" They will not coddle or baby you. They *will* call a spade a f------ shovel, and they *will* tell you the truth whether you want to hear it or not, and they *will* teach you the Mysteries of the Universe!

The most fascinating thing about these Goddesses and Gods is the devotion they inspire in those who come to know them. If you come to know any of Them, you'll understand, and the devotion you feel will be inspired by love, not fear.

To get back to Bast, and my experience with Her—I realized very quickly that I was dealing with a Dark Lady. I had been asked once what Goddess of another pantheon would I compare Bast to, and out of my mouth came "Hecate." I asked Bast if this had been accurate.

"Yes," came the answer, "but I am golden, where She is silver." Hecate is lunar; Bast, solar.

I then asked if, as we believed, the cat was the proper animal to connect with Her. Again, She agreed, but pointed out that it was not the domestic cat, but one I have heard called a "jungle cat." (Very probably one of the African wild cats, possibly *felis capensis*.)

When I receive information in such a meditation, I do not accept it as fact without verification. I make a note of it, and either research, where possible, or wait and see what comes up later. The domestic cat was not known in Egypt until the 12th Dynasty. If you will look at the statues from earlier dynasties, you will note the differences: longer ears, longer legs, etc.

The Lady said one other thing on this subject. Almost as an aside, She said, " . . . except in another land, where it is the wolf." I later learned of a legend in which Hecate shape-changed into a wolf.

There are reasons why animals were chosen by the ancients to represent the deities. Consider the cat for a moment. Many people don't like cats. An adult cat is aloof, and chooses the time when, place where and recipient to whom he bestows affection. You can be honored when a cat is affectionate to you. No one owns a cat. Cats are swift, silent, and deadly to their prey, yet they are warm and loving mothers, and very protective.

We once called upon Bast, using the chant described earlier, to ask Her help. Some sub-humans had tied a firecracker to the tail of a friend's cat. The poor animal was in pain, and so terrified he would not come out of hiding to let his "owners" treat the injury.

We were outside, in dark of the Moon, as we chanted. At the same moment, we all became aware of a darker area in the surrounding darkness. What we saw/felt was about 18 feet of cat, and lots of teeth and eyes. The first words out of my mouth were "Wait a minute, Lady! We didn't do it." We were also extremely glad we hadn't.

What does this say about Bast? Although She is a Dark Lady, She is also a Mother Goddess . . . loving and protective. She is not, however, a "Mommy." Her children are as quickly corrected when they misbehave as they would be protected when they wandered into danger. When she is in Mother "mode," however, She has been known to purr!

Bast in Her human-bodied form is often shown holding a sistrum. Because of this, She is sometimes considered a patron of the arts. Her response to my inquiry about this was that the arts belonged to Hat Hor. The sistrum was used to get Bast's attention.

This fits in with my feelings that the animal-headed, human-bodied form originally represented a priest or priestess. If this is indeed the case, the clothes such a figure was wearing would be red, for a Priestess of Bast was often called "The lady in the red dress."

The stones we use for Bast are obsidian, and either citrine, cat's eye or tiger's eye. The various types of obsidian are often found connected with Dark Deities, because working with it has the effect of reflecting truth, whether you want it or not, whether you like it or not. The other stones, of course, reflect her eyes.

We call on Bast for any work which involved cats, of course, but she is more than a Cat Goddess. You can call upon her for protection, or guidance. (Remember, She'll tell you the truth, even if you don't want to hear it.) The cat's ability to strike with claws extended or not symbolizes two possible courses of action. You can ask Her what course to take, if any.

She can, of course, be your High Goddess, if you see all the others within Her. She is that to a friend of mine who often refers to Her as "Momcat."

Do not fear what Bast or the other Dark Ladies and Lords have to teach you. Magical paths are those on which we seek truth and growth. You will always get that from Them, especially if you are willing to learn what They have to teach.

Goddess if you will it so
Help us learn what we must know
If our spirits are to grow
MAU BAST

RA

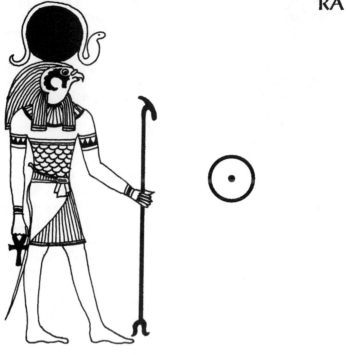

*Brightly He shines,
the Golden One!*

My first contact with Ra was not a pleasant one. He was angry, and, although I was not the object of His anger, (thank goodness) it was a frightening experience. He's very powerful, of course, and I would not want to be the one who had caused His displeasure.

A while ago, a sad incident occured in our community. A student in a Craft group had been physically abused by the High Priest and High Priestess, something that horrified the rest of us, not only for her sake, but also for the sake of the community and the Craft. Most members of our community are hard-working, devout Witches, and to have two group leaders use their office to abuse a student in the name of the God and Goddess enraged and disgusted us. The fact that they admitted the act, and believed they were perfectly within their rights to do what they'd done, was nauseating and frightening. (The Craft has enough troubles without its members using it to exercise their own sicknesses in its name.)

That incident was not actively in my thoughts at the time, however. The weather had been overcast and damp until this afternoon. As I walked, the Sun was warm on my face, and I was singing Ra's name in my mind.

Suddenly, I felt His Presence—powerful and angry—and I heard: "**Now** you call my name?"

"Yes, Lord, but . . . "

"One of my children has been injured and you called not my name?"

"No, Lord, but . . . " I wanted to say that the group involved was Celtic, and it just hadn't occurred to me to call upon this particular Lord. I had already called upon Asar, and Anpu, but I regret to say I hadn't thought to call upon Ra. I was given very little chance to say anything. My entire contribution to the conversation was "Yes, Lord, but . . . " and "No, Lord, but. . ."

"Know you not that all are my children?"

"Yes, Lord, but . . . "

He proceeded to tell me exactly what He felt about the matter, and what He intended to do about it. His actions would apparently not be immediate.

"They will go through the darkness," He told me, "and it will be terrible. But they will long for that darkness when they meet my flame!"

I confess to have smiled at that moment. It was not, I'm sure, a pleasant smile. Realizing that ultimately these two would pay for their act against their student, the Craft, and the Gods, was a matter of delight to me. Although most of the community officially dissociated from this coven (a few thought whatever they did was all right because the two people said it was part of their tradition) we've kept an eye on them. Nothing horrible has happened to them yet, but I have full faith that they will learn the lessons needed when they face this Lord.

What did I learn from this contact with Ra? Among other things, He is very protective of all of us, He is angered by those who hurt us, and that I wouldn't want to be on His bad side.

Ra represents the physical aspects of the Sun, those we can sense—light and heat. In the New Kingdom of Tamera, His name and attributes were combined with those of another Sun God, Amen, and called Amen-Ra.

While I don't use this name, I understand the combination. Amen represents the invisible aspects of the Sun, the ultraviolet rays and so forth.

The Tamerans pictured Ra sailing across the sky in a bark, beginning the day as a youth and aging as the journey went on. Nut swallowed Him at Sunset and gave birth to Him at dawn.

There are many Sun deities in Tameran mythology. Groups or individuals who wish to work with Tameran deities just have to choose which they will work with and see as the Sun.

Sothistar uses four to represent the Sun both in its daily and annual cycles: Khephera is the Sun at midnight and at Yule, both times of unseen beginnings. Heru sa Aset, the Younger, is the Sun at dawn and at Spring. Ra is the Sun at noon and midsummer. Tum is the Sun at evening and Autumn. Ra, like several other deities, was often portrayed as a Hawk. This bird soars above all free, and powerful, and all-seeing.

To some, Ra was (and is) the mightiest Lord of all. Although He is not, to me, the High Lord, He has my respect and love.

Hail, Ra! Ever blessed be!

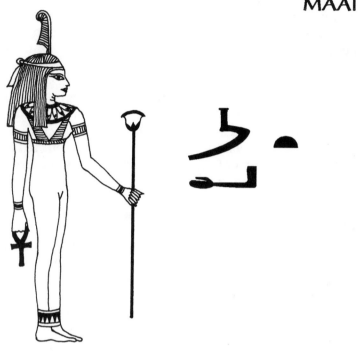

*To understand Maat,
balance a feather on its tip in the
palm of your hand.*

The above comes from a paper written by Qeshet. There is more to the paper, but that one sentence told me that he had indeed studied and worked with this Lady and gotten to know Her.

Her Name means "Truth," and "Justice," each difficult words to define. We all have our own definitions, our own ideas of what Truth and Justice are. They can both mean "that which is right."

The Egyptians taught that everyone had his or her own Maat. In this sense, She represents the right way for you to go, your integrity, the right thing to do.

Her symbol is a red ostrich feather, according to various sources. My meditations and work have revealed that, although the ostrich feather is perfectly good, almost any feather will serve as a focal point.

A feather is light and delicate. It is also very strong for its size. Feathers keep birds warm, and make it possible for them to fly. An owl feather would be a wonderful symbol for Maat because of the owl's silent flight; silent, as Truth often is, having no need to shout.

An owl feather would be perfect, if it were legal to own one. However, our country has very strict laws for the protection of our winged cousins. Because I am in favor of protecting them, I urge you to obey the laws. All migratory birds are protected and it is illegal to own any part of them. There are feathers that are legal, some of the ostrich's among them.*

Take any wing feather and move it through the air. Feel the pressure of the air against it. You can't see the air, but it is there. So is Maat always present, although not necessarily visible.

In my coven, we have a special feather consecrated to Maat, as Her Feather. As did the ancients, we take any important vow holding this feather, and we swear "by the Feather of Maat."

There is another magical use for an ostrich feather that you might like. For very special writing, signing oaths, or even your Book of Shadows, you can make a feather pen. Soak the quill in vinegar, and when it has softened, force the base of a pen nib into it. Let it dry and harden. You can reinforce the quill with yarn or narrow ribbon. Ask Maat to bless your pen, and all that you will write with it.

Maat is not a creatrix—only lies must be created. The truth already exists.

Maat is the pattern of the universe, unfolding as it should. One of the times we feel the most despair is when events make us feel alone, apart, no longer part of the pattern. Be assured that Maat always exists, Her pattern always is. You can only cease to be part of it by your own choice.

She is the Tao, She is Integrity. She is the tap root we each have connecting us with the life force, with the Gods. If we go against that which is right often enough, we break that connection. In so doing, we lose the energy we receive, the direction, the love. She does not abandon us, we abandon Her. I do not, however, believe this would be permanent. No matter how we tangle the thread of our lives. She

---

*While it's true that Fish and Game doesn't have the time or personnel to come after any of us for possessing one father, why break the law? I hardly think it would be an act of which this Goddess would approve.

who is the pattern will find a way to weave us back into our proper places in the tapestry.

It is to this Lady you should apply to know the right thing to do. Be warned, however. Your answer will not have to do with right on a short-term basis. It will be right from the point of view of your destiny, all your lives, in striving to be one with the God and Goddess. It will usually be the hardest thing to do, and you are not likely to see immediate results.

One magical method of working with Maat is suggested in J. Murray Hope's PRACTICAL EGYPTIAN MAGIC. When you are in doubt about a person, a situation, or a course of action, you can weigh him, her or it on the Scales of Maat.

Visualize the hand-held scales before you. Hold the handle, feel the weight of the scales. One side holds the feather of Maat. On the other, you visualize an image of the person, or a symbol of your question. Lift your hand, and the scales, asking Her help. Hold the scales up until you "feel" them taken from you. Your answer will come in the next several days.

She is not a Goddess who is easy to know well, not a personal Goddess. Why? After all, we value truth—what better Goddess to serve?

Truth, that which is right, is so much more vast that we can encompass, so much more than we can imagine, than we can understand. She sees all time as one—all our lives as a continuity. What might seem horribly wrong, terribly unjust from our limited view might be, from Her point of view, exactly what should be.

Lies of any sort were anathema in Tamera. All right-thinking citizens of the Two Lands hoped that in the eternal records Tehuti would put these words after their name: *maat kheru*, "whose word is truth."

There did not seem to be a cultic center for this Lady. While we can find no records of priests or priestesses of Maat, I know she has at least one now. You could do far worse than choose to serve Maat. As I said before, we each have our own Maat and we should each serve her in that respect. Though we might be priest or priestess of another deity, of another pantheon, it would behoove all of us, if we tried to live our lives guided by the Lady whose name means Truth, if we, too lived so that Tehuti would say of us "Their words are truth."

Anubis and Horus

ANPU (Anubis)

Do you dare to walk the hidden ways?
Do you dare to face the jackal?

Jackals—scavengers—night prowlers—altogether nasty animals, right? And you probably aren't going to listen to any talk about the necessity of scavengers in the scheme of things.

Did you know that jackals are as often hunters as scavengers? They usually mate for life. They have a very strong family unit. It is not unusual for half-grown pups to baby-sit while the parents are hunting. I have seen films of two young jackals taking on a hyena five times their size to protect their younger brothers and sisters.

Loyalty and courage are not such horrible qualities, are they? Instead, they are a standard often hard to live up to, a standard that can present quite a challenge.

Anpu is the Guardian, the Guide, the Challenger, the Dark Lord. To pass His challenge, you must be possessed of courage. You must

be ready to face Him steadfastly, or you will not learn the tremendous amount He has to teach.

In most legends, Anpu is the son of Asar and Nebet Het. He
assists Asar, the Judge, in judging the dead. You'll often find him
portrayed in scenes which depict the "Weighing of the Heart,"
another challenge.

It is He who serves as a Guide through the Underworld—jackals are very good in the dark.

I've gotten to know Anpu quite well. My husband and High
Priest, Chris, is His Priest. Although Chris was chosen by Anpu
rather than the other way around, the association is certainly appropriate. Chris has an unerring sense about people. If there is something wrong about a person, he knows it. He is the only person in
our coven who can veto the entrance of a potential student. Chris
was, for a long time, the Guardian of our coven. A priest of Anpu
is most appropriate for this office.

According to some sources, the priest/esses of Anpu were the
true-seers. We are told that lying was an anathema to this God.

Anpu is an observer, a reporter. In a meditation, He once said to
me, "If you are afraid, reach out into the darkness. Feel the darkness
gather around your hand, and I will remove your fear."

He does not remove your fear from you, but removes you from
your fear, lets you step back and view it objectively, so that you can
do what you need to handle the situation. If he removed your fear,
you would not necessarily be able to do that. There are times when
not being afraid would be stupid. Lack of fear is not courage.
Courage is being afraid and going ahead and doing what you must.
There is a big difference.

His stone is an apache tear, a form of obsidian that appears
opaque until it is held up against the light. Its effects are somewhat
gentler that other forms of obsidian, but they can still be difficult to
deal with: obsidian will tell you the truth always, and we are not
always ready to face the truth.

Some years ago, we had a teacher in our community who shared
her knowledge about crystals and stones. From her I learned most
of what I know about the subject. It was she who taught us that
obsidian must be worked with carefully, and that not everyone is
ready to work with it.

Naturally, lots of people were absolutely sure they were worthy and ready and mature, and they rushed out to by obsidian balls without giving it a second thought. Some of them were ready, but most of them weren't. I can see the effects. Because they weren't ready, they don't believe the things the stone has told them, and much has been happening in their lives to show that they are doing anything they can to ignore the truth. Goddess guide them. They'll need it.

We've worked with His protective aspect more than once. Our community had some problems with certain members sending out negativity. We needed to protect our homes and ourselves from that. With the help of Anpu, four of us charged some apache tears to a very special purpose: they were charged to rebound any negativity sent toward us, and to turn any negativity we might send out into love and light.

We gave the apache tears to anyone who might be a target of the negativity. We all carried them and several were placed around various homes.

A week later, the woman we believed to be the source of the negativity started complaining that some opals she owned were full of negative feelings. She couldn't understand it. (Three of those apache tears were in the pockets of people around her at the moment.) I learned later that she and her students worked for weeks trying to track the negativity back to its source, to see who was sending it. Naturally she failed, since she was the source.

If you are unfamiliar with the ethics of magical practice, you may have learned a thing or two from this story. We did not attack. That would have been a serious mistake. More than once I've believed the source of problems was a particular person, and was wrong. If I had performed a spell against that person, I would have been doing the wrong thing. We simply sent back the negativity that was sent our way, and prevented any of our own negativity from going out. The lady received back only what she had sent.

Another protection we received from Anpu had to do with our home. We'd been burglarized four times, and were, understandably, a little tired of it. I took a suggestion from Murray Hope's *PRACTICAL EGYPTIAN MAGIC*, and everyday when I left the house, I would say, "Lord Anpu, please guard our home."

After about a month, as I was leaving the house, I repeated the line as usual, and heard very distinctly, "I'm guarding already!" From that day on, I said, "Lord Anpu, thank you for guarding our home."

One possibility mentioned in Hope's book has certainly occurred more than once at our house, and at the houses of others who've used the same protection: black dogs keep showing up, not every day, but often enough to be noticeable.

Although the jackal is the animal normally attributed to Anpu, and the one that is, as I've shown, most appropriate, there is some question among archaeologists as to whether this is correct—they see him as a dog, a wolf, or a jackal. When Anpu came to my husband in visions, He came as both a jackal and a wolf.

There is another deity, Apuat, portrayed exactly as Anpu except that He is colored gray instead of black. He was the High God in the city the Greeks called "Lycopolis," meaning "City of the Wolf."

Both the jackal and the wolf have undeserved reputations. Although I love the jackal as a symbol, you might be more comfortable working with the wolf at first.

You have nothing to fear from Anpu if you are ready to walk the hidden ways, if you are ready to face the hidden truths, if you have courage. Passing His challenge is reason to be proud. If you are not yet ready, however, there is no reason to be ashamed. You will always have another chance.

And when you are ready, and do pass the challenge, you will make an amazing discovery: Anpu isn't black and snarling at all. He is shining gold!

Can you bear to face the hidden truth?
Can you bear to face the jackal?

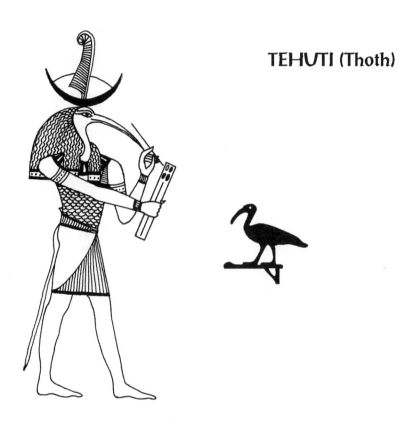

TEHUTI (Thoth)

Head of an ibis, eyes of a sage
Wisest of all wise ones, holiest mage

It seems difficult, at first, to look at the strange figure with human body and bird head with long curved beak and hold any serious thoughts. It can seem even laughable to consider this figure the Lord of Wisdom.

Yet, if you will meditate upon Him, imagine Him standing before you in this form, and look into those eyes, you will not find Him ludicrous. You will be entranced by the wisdom, and, yes, humor, you find in those eyes of infinite depth.

Knowledge, Wisdom, Words, Books, Science, Learning, Teaching—all these are His, all these are represented by Him. He is also ruler of knowledge beyond "book-learning." He holds the keys to the greater mysteries.

Many believe the hieroglyphs are some of those keys. Tehuti is said to be the Inventor of this alphabet. Just as many believe the Tarot deck to be a book of knowledge hidden in symbolism, so do many believe that there is more to the hieroglyphs than representation of sounds.

This pictographic alphabet was called by the ancients *medu neter*, "words of the God." This name revealed, as names often do, the feelings the Ancients had for their alphabet. I am sure there is much to be learned from their study.

When we did a contact ritual on Tehuti, the words given to each of us were different.

To me, He said: "Teach what you teach. Prepare them for me."

To another writer, He said "The papyrus on which I write must be fine and smooth; the brush well made; the ink finely ground."

To a man involved with computers, He said: "There is information that must be in your memory banks before I can teach you."

Although each message was different, there was a thread that ran through all the messages. As Ember put it, that thread was, "Pardon me, but this is a graduate course."

In order to learn the greater mysteries Tehuti can teach you, you must prepare to be ready for that knowledge. You must be worthy of His teachings. You must advance spiritually, strive for growth, reach for the knowledge you need.

Tehuti will, of course, help you to achieve this. The important thing you must have is a sincere, soul-deep desire to learn and grow. Without it, no amount of study will help you. The desire is important, but remember Tehuti is also interested in your spiritual growth as well as your mental development.

He has so *much* to teach you, and he will do whatever is necessary to help you learn. In at least one case, His appearance changed to a form to which a specific person could relate. One of my former students was a bluegrass musician. Tehuti appeared to him wearing mirror-shades and helped with musical arrangements.

Funny? Maybe. Irreverent? Who am I to tell a God how He shall appear? My student loved this God most dearly. He had a personal relationship with Tehuti. That's the important thing.

Tehuti was very special to ancient scribes. Every morning, a scribe's first act was to make a libation to this Lord by dropping a few drops on the ground from the water bowl used for ink.

The current equivalent of a scribe might be a secretary, a book-keeper, or a writer. I use a computer to write, and have no water bowl from which to libate. I make an offering from my first cup of coffee! For me, this beverage is a necessary working tool.

That may sound frivolous, but I make my libation with all rev-erence, asking Tehuti to bless the work I am to do that day. I have never had the feeling He thought my act was irreverent.

You needn't be a writer, secretary or bookkeeper to honor Tehuti. You need only have the desire to learn and grow, and the willing-ness to work at achieving those things. Such hard work will always be rewarded by the Lord of Wisdom.

As a teacher, I call upon Tehuti often for His guidance in serving my students. This Lord is the greatest teacher of all, and He has helped me uncounted times to teach and lead my students correctly. The current members of Sothistar are very hard-working and have advanced wonderfully during their training. Much of the credit for their growth must, of course, go to each of them because they've worked hard. Any credit Chris and I are due must be shared with this Wise Lord. We could not have done it without his help.

If you wish to learn from Tehuti, work hard and reach for His Knowledge. He can teach you so much more than any earthly teacher. This does not mean, if you have a human teacher, that what he or she has to offer is unimportant. Learn from your teacher, build a foundation of knowledge, and then Tehuti will teach you. His is not a basic course—it's an advanced one.

Oh, I would learn from Thee!
I would earn wings!

Nut and Geb

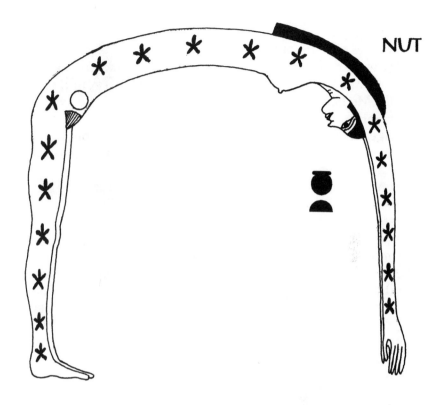

I can see high above
How you cover all the world with your love

"Mother . . ..grandmother . . .a cool hand soothing a fevered fore-head." These words are Ember's, from a paper she about the Lady Nut.

This Goddess is pictured, traditionally, as the night sky, as a woman curved over the horizon with Her Feet to the East and Her Hands to the West. The stars jewel Her Body, and the Milky Way flows from Her Breast. When Sothistar casts a circle, we visualize Her stretched over us.

Legend says Her lover was Geb, the Earth God, and She gave birth to Aset, Asar, Nebet Het, Her Ur and Set.

She is Mother of the Gods, ancient and yet not old. The feeling you have in Her Presence is of agelessness. She has known pain and learned to live with it. She has watched eons pass beneath Her. She has watched empires rise and fall, civilizations grow and crumble.

She surrounds us with her love, hurts when we hurt, weeps for us, rejoices with us, and eternally holds us in her womb

We invoked Her "by accident" one night. Instead of spoken invocation, Chris began to sing "Ancient Mother," a beautiful chant by Brooke Medicine Eagle. The Goddess who appeared was wonderful. Her Presence touched us all, especially Ember.

Eager to learn more about this Lady, Ember wrote down the chant, made sure she knew the tune, and went home to work with this Lady further.

Some months later we did an invocation of Nut. We all recognized Her as the same Goddess we'd met before. Ember is now Her Priestess.

In hieroglyphs, Her name is spelled with a small round ceramic pot and the symbol for "feminine"—a container and woman—and like so many hieroglyphs, this expresses its meaning so well, so beautifully. As Mother of the Gods, She contains all of us, all our Earth, all that lives. She is Mother, true, but more Grandmother. She is able to view our temper tantrums and hurt feelings with a bit more objectivity than a new mother would. She knows the painful times are often lessons, and that we must suffer to learn them. She also knows we could have learned them more easily if we weren't so stubborn and sometimes, so blind. If we falter, she will pick us up, dust us off, and send us right back into the fray, lovingly, but brooking no nonsense. She would never consider letting us give up.

If you would come to know this beautiful Lady, go out on a clear night and look up at the starry sky. There She will be. See her above you. Feel Her above you, know that She loves you.

Although they are rarely pictured in paintings I've seen, and seldom mentioned in any ancient writings, more than one member of my group has felt that Nut has night-dark night-soft wings enfolding us all. You may feel those wings about you. If you wish, speak a prayer found on one of the shrines in the tomb of Tutankamen:

Mother Nut, spread Thy wings over me, encircle me with Thy arms in health and life that I may be inside Thee, that Thou mayest be my protection.

Her Love is unconditional. Nothing is hidden from Her, She can see all. She knows your vices and your virtues, your triumphs and your failures. She knows even those things you hide from yourself.

And She loves you. If you feel that love, you will find it impossible not to return it.

As a symbol of Nut, a piece of sodalite serves beautifully. This is a dark blue stone with white markings—the night sky and the stars that are its jewels. Not only does it resemble Her body, but the feeling I get from it is very much the feeling I get from Her. It can absorb my confusion, help my order my thoughts, and feel I can handle any problem.

We know, all of us, that the night sky is not solid, and that the stars are not only billions of miles away from us, but often of miles away from each other, even those who appear in groupings we call constellations. We know that, and yet that does not keep us from seeing Nut when we stand outside and gaze at the star-jeweled sky. If She contains all those stars, she is truly Mother of the Gods, Womb of Creation.

I can see, with my heart,
Thou art beautiful to see,
oh, Thou art!

Lord of the Earth
and the plains
and the highest mountain

Near my house, there are cliffs jutting up through the earth, thrusting up into the sky. Each time I see them, I think of this Lord, and say a word of praise to Him. It was in these huge rocks that I first saw Him, and came to know a Lord not many are privileged to know.

I can feel His strength by placing my hand on a sun-warmed boulder. He is Father of the Gods, the foundation on which they and we stand. We cannot imagine ignoring Him, or failing to know Him.

Beloved of Nut, Father of Her children, He is the stability of the Earth under our feet, the strength of the Earth people in my part of the world may know better than most, because we can feel that tremendous strength when large portions of the Earth move.

When we cast a circle, we picture this God stretched beneath us, as we picture Nut stretched above us. We are held between Them, Mother and Father, Grandmother and Grandfather, safe, protected, loved.

There are those who have trouble with the idea of an Earth God and a Sky Mother. An Earth Mother seems much easier to understand because it is in the Earth we plant seeds to grow.

Consider the Earth, however, as a seed in the womb of Nut, the Sky Mother. Why can't our planet be both Mother and Father? As complex as life is, we'd be foolish to restrict our ideas to one level, to one point of view. The gods are complex beyond our ken, and we must stretch to try to achieve that understanding. The very stretching is part of our development whether we reach that understanding or not.

With that in mind, spend some time seeing the Earth as Geb. I heartily recommend this, because you will come to know this glorious Lord, and He is worth knowing. You will also learn much about the Earth if you'll try to feel it as a Father. Try feeling it as both and see the difference.

Striving to know Geb is more than an exercise. He is an aspect of the God many people don't know for the very reason that we tend to gravitate toward the Earth Mother. He does exist. He is real. He is of the Earth. He is of us, and we can't afford to ignore any part of ourselves, much less any part of the God.

Geb will give you strength if you need it. He can bring you stability. You stand between His Body and that of his Beloved Lady, Nut, in the love that flows between them. Know that, stand there and feel that, and you will never again feel alone.

Honor Him by caring for the Earth. Send him your love when you see the towering cliffs. Feel his power rising up through your feet. Lie on a huge boulder and feel his strength and His Love. Feel yourself sinking into the Earth, surrounded by his glory. You'll never regret it. I never have.

Lord of the Earth, praise to Thee!

Called a dwarf by those who have not learned to see.

This strange little dwarf, sometimes gleeful, sometimes fiercely brandishing a dagger, is one of the few Tameran Gods ever depicted full-face. What does this mean? I haven't the foggiest, but I'm sure there is a reason. I can think of only one other deity so portrayed, a Goddess who was adopted from another country. It is said that Bes is also an import.

There is always a reason for Egyptian symbolism. Portraying deities in profile could imply that They have two aspects. Conversely, portraying a subject full face could mean that there is a hidden aspect. If you wish a subject for meditation, here's a subject for you. That meditation will be most meaningful if you'll do it now before reading on. You can then compare your ideas with ours.

Bes

Bes is short, deformed, ugly to look upon, and very dear to my coven. He is a God of protection, childbirth, and humor. It is that last which makes him most dear to us. The last thing we do in a Moon Rite is called "The Four Fold Feast." By the time we begin this feast, we have done our magical work, spoken with the Goddess and or God, worshipped and praised Them. During our Four Fold Feast, we begin to wind down, to come back to Earth, to prepare for the ending ritual and returning to the mundane world.

A symbol of each element is blessed and passed around the circle. As each passes the symbol to the next, a wish is made for the person receiving the symbol. For example, someone might pass the Air symbol and say, "May it lighten your burdens."

At some point during this feast, something strange will happen. Something unexpected will come out of someone's mouth. Once, when the symbol for earth was a bran muffin, one of our people handed it to the next, smiled sweetly and said, "May it bring you movement."

The reaction to such a remark is usually "He's hee—re." We laugh, and welcome Bes to our circle. If he doesn't appear, we worry. He never seems to mind when we attribute smart-aleck remarks to Him.

I've heard Bes referred to as the Egyptian Pan, and I do find some truth to that. Both are Gods of joy and fun. Pan is known as the Protector of the Greenwood, and Bes does have his protective aspects— although these are more often related to the home. In Tamera, His image was found on bedposts, cosmetic pots, hair brushes and mirrors.

It may be that His ugly face scared away evil spirits, much the same as the Egyptian gargoyles. Yet, although I've seen very little of His protective aspects, I have the feeling that He'd be anything but laughable.

His role in birth seems to be two-fold: He does serve to keep evil spirits away, but He also encourages the child to be born: "Come on! It's fun! Hurry up!"

Work with Bes can teach you the deeper meanings of laughter, of jokes, of humor. Many people have the idea that humor is frivolous. They are very wrong. It is one of the essentials of life, physical, emotional and spiritual. It can mean survival.

One of the underlying themes of the TV series "M.A.S.H." was that the craziness that the characters indulged in was necessary to keep them sane. Anyone who has ever worked in a high tension job can understand that.

When we did our meditation on Bes, a good friend who is a registered nurse recalled a time early in her career when she and others were working frantically to keep a two-year old child alive.

As the tension built, as they worked harder and harder, the jokes started. They were horrible, obsene, black humor—and they were necessary to help the doctors and the nurses continue. If they had not been able to release some of the tension, they would not have been able to continue their desperate work. The jokes kept them from screaming.

I worked with the police department for many years and have seen similar situations, made horrible jokes that would be obscene to those who weren't involved.

If you haven't ever been in such an intense situation, have you ever made a joke because you were embarrassed? Multiply that need a thousand-fold.

Bes teaches us to laugh at our own frailties, to accept them, and quit berating ourselves for having them.

By portraying Bes as a dwarf, the Tamerans may have acknowledged humankind's usual derogation of humor, accepting the unthinking point of view that laughter is trivial. Only those who came to know this God and His hidden meanings learned the truth, that He is a giant when you know and value what He has to teach.

Qeshet, who at this time is acting Guardian of our coven, is also an inveterate punster, as is Chris, my husband. The combination of Guardian and comedian struck us as an interesting combination and we jokingly suggested that he become a priest of Bes. Our research hadn't shown any cultic center or priesthood of Bes, and Ember, Qeshet's wife, ventured the opinion that if such priests made puns, they were probably killed before puberty. (She and I have always felt that we were building karmic credit by not killing our husbands when they made horrible wordplay.)

Bes also reminds us that the besr protection and defense against black magic is laughter. Someone who would take the time and energy to use the energies of magic to do harm to others—when he or she could do such glorious things with it—even for his or her own benefit—is laughable, and should be regarded as an object of scorn, not fear. Robert Anton Wilson once compared doing black magic to using Shakespeare's first folio for toilet paper. Isn't that funny? Couldn't you laugh at someone that stupid?

If you and/or your group have reason to believe you are the subject of black workings you can call upon Bes to help you protect yourselves. Obtain either a picture of the person doing the evil magic (if you know who it is), or obtain some item to serve as a symbol of that person. Place it in the center of the circle. Ask Bes to join you in the circle. Chant his name, if you wish. When you feel his presence, begin to discuss the person who is working against you. Think about how ridiculous he or she is being.

Talk about the ignorance shown by this person who obviously does not realize that he or she will receive back three-fold what is being sent out. Do anything and everything to make yourselves see the humor of the situation. Do anything you can to make yourselves laugh at him/her and at yourselves for worrying about it. Bes will help you.

Laughter is the best defense against fear. You just cannot be afraid of anyone or anything that you can laugh at.I have no medical proof, but I truly believe that the physical act of laughter is healing, beyond its ability to relieve tension.

Bes teaches us to laugh at our own foibles, and to forgive ourselves for them. He teaches us to accept ourselves and stop putting ourselves down for being human. I'm reminded of the time when, at 14, I was sent to bed without supper. Although I was slender, I was healthy and in no danger of starving to death before breakfast. Oh, but at that age, we all suffer so well, and everything is a matter of life and death. So I took the birdseed from my parakeet, shelled it, and mashed it into a glass with some water. I ate it! And suffered so wonderfully!

I laugh at that now, but it seemed so deadly serious at the time. Bes teaches us to see these things in their true light, to laugh at them, and love ourselves the better for having been human. He gives us the hope that someday, we may be able to laugh lovingly at the things we are taking so seriously now.

Bes is also the jester, the court fool, who is usually anything but a fool.

The more we work with this God, the less we see His ugliness, and the more we see His beauty; the less we see that He is a dwarf, and the more we see the strength that comes from Him. We've come to believe His importance has been highly underrated, and plan to give Him more honor than we already do.

We will honor him by treasuring our laughter, by recognizing its value, and by finding more joy in the lives we live.

And yes, Qeshet did dedicate to Bes, joyfully and full of knowledge of the work it would take to serve this Mighty Lord!

Bes is a giant to me!

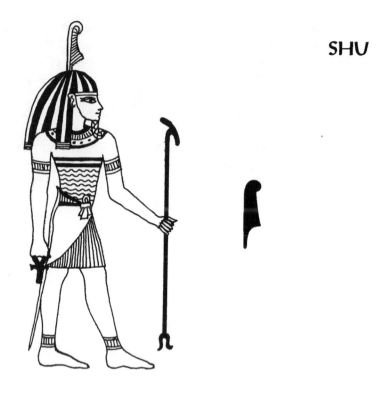

Take a deep slow breath, trying to feel the air entering your lungs. Hold it there a moment. Remember that the air you breathe is a part of the atmosphere covering our planet. As you exhale, whisper the sound "Shhhh" and toward the end of the breath, change to a whispered "uuu."

Be aware of the air around you, touching every inch of your body.

Think on the wind in all its aspects, from the gentlest breeze to gale force. "Listen" to it. Try to hear the God's name. "Shu."

Visualize the planet Earth hanging in space. See the atmosphere that surrounds it. See the movement of the winds, the air around the entire sphere, all connected, flowing from one direction to another, surrounding our home.

All of these are Shu. He is around you, within you. He enters your body with each breath, bringing you life, and exits it with each exhalation, taking away that which is poison to you. He enters and exits through your pores as well.

The trees show his passing. The birds soar through and upon Him. Whitecaps reveal His presence on the sea. The movement of air around our planet are His presence. Shu is all of these.

His symbol is the ostrich feather. Waving such a feather slowly through the air gives a wonderful visual awareness of His presence.

Although this is the deity we call at the East for Air, Shu is more properly the God of the atmosphere. On a physical level, however, our atmosphere is the air of which we are most aware, so His connection with this element is appropriate.

If I had to chose one word to describe Him, it would be "movement." We usually become consciously aware of Him only when He moves, and often not even then. How often are you aware of the movement of air in and out of your lungs?

As I write this, my household is very much aware of air and its movement. We are in the midst of a season of windstorms—60 to 80 mile-an-hour winds. Outside, we feel it, and see its effects. Inside, we hear it, constantly.

From time to time we've muttered prayers, asking Shu to take it easy before the roof of the carport ends up in San Diego.

Yet we are aware that Shu is present not only in the winds buffeting our home. He is all the Air in the atmosphere all around us, and that atmosphere is in constant movement. He is not only a part of it, He is it.

My knowledge of Shu's nature is one reason I hesitate to do any kind of weather magic. All weather on our planet is interconnected. Effecting a change in the weather near me could adversely effect weather elsewhere, and that would be my responsibility. Magic works that way.

A young friend of mine in Florida wrote to me some years ago about the success she and friends had had in turning a hurricane away from their city. The hurricane had indeed turned, and hit a major city. If my friend is responsible, I hope the people in that city deserved the damage done by that storm. If not, my friend has a lot to answer for.

The truth is, Shu isn't concerned with an individual windstorm or hurricane. It is the whole that is His concern.

As is the case with Maat, Shu is somewhat impersonal with regard to human concerns. (We have found this true of all four deities we call for the elements.)

It isn't that He is uncaring, but simply that his point of view is such much more vast than ours. The Gods know our current incarnations are temporary and our eternal spirits cannot be destroyed.

Shu does project a feeling of affection for us. I've felt it. Ember put it this way, "Do you like bubbles? They are beautiful, and you love them, but you aren't upset when they break."

Our current incarnations are just beautiful bubbles to Shu. He loves us, but isn't upset when the thin shell surrounding us breaks. We still exist.

Although individual storms and so forth are not matters of concern to Shu, air pollution certainly is; it desecrates His body.

Of course, Air is more than physical air, and so is Shu. He is beginnings, and potential, light, freedom and movement. He is inspiration. He is aspiration, reaching for the stars.

We have a beautiful yellow ostrich feather that is our Shu symbol, and I love to hold it up and watch it react to the slightest movement of the air in the room. I become aware that Shu is always present, inside us and out. He is a necessity to life, ever-changing, ever the same. Shu also reminds us of his vastness with the thought of this fact, that the air we breathe now, is the same air that has been breathed throughout mankind's existence. That molecule entering your lungs as you read may have entered the lungs of Aristotle, Beethoven, or Rameses the Second. What a thought!

Be aware of Shu in the breeze, in the storm, in the fragrance of flowers, in the tornado, and the "dust devil" you see. (Dust, by the way, is the closest we can come to a proper stone for Him.) He is in and about you, sustaining your life.

If you would honor Him, one way is to be careful what you say. Words are given sound by breath. Do not use the body of this Lord to curse or cause pain. Do no use His Body to speak untruths.

Another way is to care for birds who travel so easily through the Lord. Feed them, provide water for them, and glory in their beauty as they fly. When you see any bird soaring, think of Shu, honor Him in your heart, and thank Him for all He gives us.

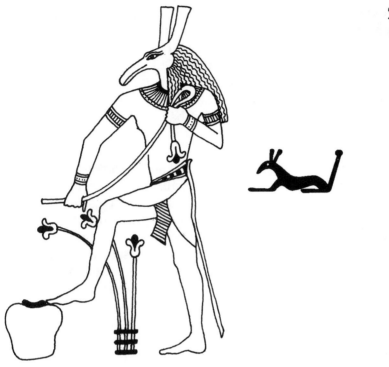

Comes the desert wind!
Comes the desert storm!

If you are familiar with Tameran mythology at all, you know the legend of Asar and Aset. (If not, it appears later in this book.) They ruled Egypt together, and their brother, Set, was jealous. He killed Asar, and sent his body, nailed into a coffin, down the Nile. Aset searched, found the body, and recovered it. While she went for help, Set found the body, and cut it into fourteen pieces and scattered the pieces over the world.

Again, the grieving goddess searched for the pieces of her husband, and established a temple each place she found a part. Once all were found, she placed them together, and with her mighty magic, not only brought new life to Asar, but conceived Heru as well.

63

Bad, nasty, evil Set! An Egyptian Satan!

Now you know, as a good pagan I can't accept that. We witches have no need for evil gods. There must be more to it than that—myths *mean* something beyond the story. I confess to you, I don't know yet the meaning of every part of the myth, but I do understand what Set represents in terms of Qabala.*.

I've tried to include as few qabalistic references as possible in this book, because this one isn't about Qabala, but I can't avoid it here. I hope this discussion will make sense if you don't have knowledge of the subject.

In this story, Asar represents Chesed and its forces—the Benevolent King, the King who nurtures civilization, patron of the arts, who teaches agriculture to his people. Set represents Geburah and its energies—the warrior king, wielder of the sword, the surgeon with a scalpel. Both are necessary for balance.

Another interpretation would be to view Asar as the grain, and Set as the harvester. The grain is cut, falls, and is scattered. Nurtured by the Air (Aset) and nourished by the Water (Nebet Het), it takes root and is reborn.

Set wasn't always considered a villain in Tamera. He was originally a desert and storm god. At various times in the beloved land's history, He was honored greatly, and not as an evil god.

Even in a country as apparently enlightened as Tamera, there were people who did not understand. There are many even today who feel any event or experience that is painful or difficult is as a result of evil. Astrologically, the lessons Mars and Saturn have to teach can be very hard, very painful, and some still refer to these as "malefic" planets.

We pagans, however, have learned that real lessons are usually hard, and hard times are usually lessons. We have learned that the cycle of life includes death, and that death is necessary for rebirth. We have come to understand that breaking down is as much a part of life as building up.

Asar was the grain, and the grain must be cut down if it is to spring up anew. Aset gathered the grain, planted it, nurtured it, and

---

*If this subject is new to you, further information is available in my first book *The Goddess And The Tree* published by Llewellyn Publications.

gave it life again. That which Asar had to give was then given to the world.

We may not like storms, but the earth is often the better for their passing. The wind storms where I live are frightening, but when they pass, the air is clean, dead leaves are blown from the trees, and much of the dust and dirt is gone.

I have seen a pot, black with decades of use, made bright again by sand-blasting. Without scouring pads, we'd never get some things clean.

That which Set takes away is never essential. He removes only the temporal, only the unnecessary, only the obstacles to growth. It is our clinging to those things that make the cutting away painful.

We cannot love and honor Asar without loving and honoring Set. He is not easy to love, but learning to do so can be a giant step forward in your growth. Once you have learned to accept Him, you will find Him glorious!

Stand and face the winds
And when the storm is passed
Only the eternal will remain
In His wake!

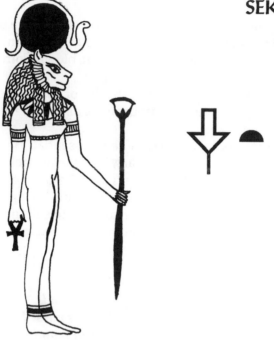

SEKHMET

A series of books I love are the *FAR MEMORY* books by Joan Grant. Four of them are set in Tamera, at three different periods in history. Ms. Grant says these books are memories of former lives.

I have no idea whether that is true. I do know the books contain many ideas I like, and hope are true, many ideals worth striving for. But there is one area where I disagree with her. She portrays both Set and Sekhmet as evil, the Egyptian equivalent of Satan.

Neither of these deities is evil. Neither of them is necessarily easy to understand, and often difficult to love.

Sekhmet's name is the feminine of the work "Sekhem" which means strength, or power. In other words, her name means "Lady of Strength," or "Lady of Power."

She is that. She is power. She is energy. She is destructive force. "AH HAH!" you say. "Destructive force! I thought you said She wasn't evil!"

She isn't. Qabalistically, she is a Geburic force just as Set is. In case, however, you are not familiar with Qabala, I'll explain. Our modern society views destruction as evil. Construction is good. Destruction is evil. To most people in our culture, it's that simple, that black and white.

Of course, it isn't, is it? Construction is not good if what you're building is a body 75 pounds overweight. Destruction is not evil if you're tearing down a building that has become unsafe. Construction is not good if what is growing is a cancer. Destruction is not evil if what is being removed is a cancer.

Sekhmet represents a destructive force that breaks down what is temporal. That which is eternal is never destroyed. As a Solar Goddess, She burns away excess.

She can be frightening. Power is often frightening, especially to those who don't understand it. It can be exhilarating when you realize that however little we like what They do, the power of the Gods is always on our side.

The Tamerans believed She was capable of causing plague, and She therefore was capable of curing it. In a different way, we do the same thing. We use vaccinations, a light case of the disease in question to prevent serious illnesses.

Like Bast, Sekhmet is a Dark Lady. (This is a difficult concept to accept when She is so definitely a Solar Goddess. But using the terms "Crone" or "Hag" would be just as confusing.) Some say that Sekhmet is the destructive power of the Sun, while Bast represents the nurturing, warming Sun. Interesting concept when you consider that part of the success with mummification is the heat of the Nile Valley. In this case, the Sun preserves instead of destroying.

Sekhmet is portrayed as a lioness, which at the very least reveals that the Tamerans observed nature, because the lioness is the more active hunter in that family of cats. I believe that the lion symbolized power to the people of the Nile Valley. It often signifies Fire to our minds which certainly is a perfect attribution for this Goddess.

Is Sekhmet more powerful than Bast? I don't think so. Can She be gentle and loving? Possibly. Do I wish to know Her better? Absolutely!

PTAH

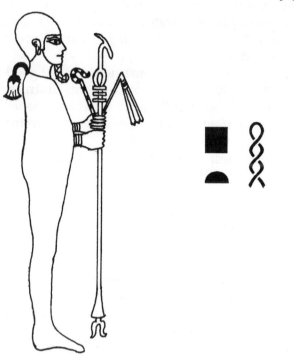

This God is usually portrayed with a smooth skull cap, his body bound in mummy wrappings. He is the God of Craftsmen. (Craftspersons, if you insist.)

When a craftsman in Tamera created a statue of a deity, he (or she) prayed to Ptah to encourage that deity to place a bit of Himself or Herself into the statue, that it might truly be worthy of honor.

You can do the same, if you are an artist. Ask, if you wish, that Ptah guide your hands that you create a statue or a picture worthy of the deity it represents. I have asked His help in writing about the Gods, that I may craft my words with such care that you will come to know and love Them as I do. We have also asked His help in painting a plaster statue, that the person's hands be guided.

His name means "force captured in form." His mummy wrappings signify the same thing. An artist controls the paints, his or her hands, any of the tools used in painting. A sculptor controls his fingers and the clay, or chisel and stone.

You can apply this to almost any job, any work. I Have a friend who is a registered nurse. She uses tools and knowledge to control germs, wounds, etc.

My husband is a prototype maker. He controls tools, both hand tools and large mills, using them and their energy to form metals and plastics.

What is your profession? A musician? A secretary? A doctor? Bulldozer driver? Bricklayer? If you'll think about it carefully, you will find that you, too, are a craftsman, that you do control some force, putting it into a desired form.

His name can be written with the symbol for heaven and the symbol for "aah" which is either a sound of praise, or the name of a moon god. Have some fun with that. You might learn more about Him in your mental meanderings.

The Tamerans were fond of word play. A word that was the reverse of another in letters might well have a reverse meaning. The word that is the reverse of ptah is "htp" (hotep or hetep). It means *peace* or *offering*. If what you offer is something you value, you could also call it a sacrifice. When an animal was offered as sacrifice, it was killed. (This occurred in many cultures.) Its life force was released to be returned to the Gods whence it came. One magical definition of sacrifice is "destroying form to release force." In this way "htp" is an opposite of "pth."

One way to contact this Lord is with soft clay. It doesn't matter whether it is clay that can be fired or not. Children's clay will serve very well. Feel the clay, shape it, squeeze it, twist it, think about its form, and, in your heart, call Ptah.

It was said that Ptah used His heart to create all that is, and so His creative power can be felt in every heart beat. You can, as you form the clay, listen for your heart beat, try to feel it. If you can, feel the power of Ptah, know that the sound and feel of your own heart is a reflection of the Gods.

He usually appears to us in a younger form than his statues show, and often in a short kilt or loin cloth. This form gives us the impression that he is more involved in the actual work of craftsmen (and women) than in simply supervising. He is not only capable of inspiring the design of a building, but also of pouring its foundation.

Portrayed as an older, experienced man, and appearing to us as a young man—what a fascinating god this is! He is one involved in all our lives, and we are blessed by His Presence.

HET HERET (Hat Hor)

Life springing from the world's heart
My Lady Het Heret, Thou art.

The first feeling you get from Her presence is that of strength—not rock hard immovable strength, but that found in nourishment, in an eternal never-ending source of life itself.

The Tamerans symbolized this by picture Het Heret as a cow, or, when she is in human form, with a crown bearing horns.

In meditation, I asked Her what stone should be used to represent Her. She said, "Hold a stone in your hand. If it says to you 'Eternity,' if it says 'strength,' it is my stone."

If any stone says that to you it will work; but for me, there is a specific one: malachite. And, as I found out later, Het Heret has been called "Lady of Malachite."

Many of the arts belong to this beautiful Goddess, but not all.
The ones that do may be any art form, if the come from the "wellsprings of the soul." (The words are Hers). This would seem to me
to include most inspired works in any form of expression—any
work that expressed a heart-felt emotion.

"Het Heret" means "House of Heaven," or "House of the Sky."
You will also see Her name spelled "Het Heru," which translates as
"House of Heru." I prefer the first. If one uses the second, however,
I believe it would refer to a god known as Her Ur (Horus the Elder),
rather than Heru son of Aset and Asar.

A symbol often connected with Het Heret is the "menat," a necklace of several strands of beads gathered into a counterpoise. This
is often shown being carried rather than worn, as a Catholic might
carry a rosary. In at least one picture, a priestess of Het Heret is
shown wearing the necklace, lifting the front as if to offer it to the
Goddess. Most of my references refer to it as a symbol of happiness
and/or a symbol of divine healing—very little else is said.

Archaeologists are probably very nice people, and no one can
deny the value of the work they've done, but they might miss something because they are not following a magical path. (If you are an
archaeologist following a magical path, I apologize.) I've found that
most of the ideas we've gained from study and meditation do not
so much contradict what the scholars and archaeologists have said,
as amplify it.

My meditations on the menat have resulted in two things the
menat could symbolize. If you have ever worn a heavy necklace or
pendant, you know how the weight felt against the back of your
neck, and can appreciate how much better it would have been if
you'd had a counterweight. Instead of all the weight being held by
your neck, the necklace would sit on your shoulders. It would be
balanced.

The Craft, qabalism, ceremonial magic—many paths recognize
the value of balance in everything. Happiness can be the result of
balance in your life. The first thing you do when you are performing
a healing on someone is to balance the energies of his or her body.

Het Heret has many attributes that seem to be in opposition —
Tree Goddess and Sky Goddess—Fertility and Music—but what
She truly represents is balance in all things. Her Strength reaches
from the depths of the Earth to the farthest reaches of the stars.

My meditations have produced another reason for the menat. The counterpoise was usually smaller than the beads in the front, and even if the size matched, the counterpoise was hidden in the back. This makes me think of all the hidden truths, all the mysteries that cannot be taught, cannot be written in books, or told in lectures. They are every bit as important (have as much weight) as the things that can be learned in normal ways.

Whether held or worn, presenting the menat and all its hidden symbolism would be an offering of your efforts to strive toward balance and/or to seek the hidden knowledge.

Whether the menat had this meaning for the Tamerans, I have no way of knowing. I do know this feels right on a gut level, and that's often the only way I know to judge the rightness of anything. Because it feels right, the menat has these meanings for us in Sothistar.

I call upon this beautiful Goddess when I am writing a song or a poem, and even when I'm writing books, if what I'm writing needs soul-deep inspiration, if I want my words to reach others deeply. (I am calling upon Her now.)

When we dance in a ritual, especially for the purpose of raising power, our feet strike the earth giving energy to it, and energy rises in response, filling us, adding to our own energy, until we are ready to send the power where we will, to heal or teach or help. From the depths of the earth, through the sky as we send that energy to its goal—all of that is Het Heret. She is a glorious Lady—but then all of Them are!

Stars nestled sweet on thy bough
My Lady Het Heret, art Thou!

KHONSU

My copy of the *Larousse Mythology* is an old soft-cover, in sad shape. Khonsu, son of Amun and Mut, is the reason I've refused to buy a new hard-cover. In the edition I have, there is a full-page picture of the head of a small statue that absolutely entrances me. I could no more flip past this picture without spending some time looking at it than I could resist mint chocolate chip ice cream in August. The newer editions show a side view of the entire statue.

The statue was found in the tomb of Tutankhamen, and, as is true of many statues found there, the features are Tut's. But there is something more, something different, something that enchants me. Perhaps, as legend promises, Ptah appealed to Khonsu to place a bit of Himself in the statue, and it is that I find enchanting. It is the presence of the God, not the features, that is so beautiful.

Khonsu is a Moon God, and the crown he wears reflects a very specific appearance of the moon. A crescent moon "on its back" with horns pointing up is so bright that the rest of the moon is dimly illuminated, producing the illusion that there are two moons; one a crescent, the other a full sphere. "The moon is holding itself in its arms," some say. Others see the Moon traveling in a crescent boat.

His pictures and statues also show one other symbol—the prince's lock, a long lock of hair, drawn to one side. In Tamera, it symbolized both youth and royalty.

This youth should not be taken to imply lack of wisdom. He signifies potential and beginnings, especially of cycles. He is the first day of the rest of your life.

We think of the moon cycle as going from New to New, but doesn't it just as surely go from Full to Full, or from first quarter to first quarter? From moonrise to moonrise is a cycle, just as sunrise to sunrise.

Khonsu teaches us not to feel we must always begin at the beginning. Do not say, "It is not New Moon, so I can't start anything." Don't wait until the New Year to make resolutions. Every day, every hour, every minute can be a beginning, if you need it so.

According to legend, Khonsu could also conquer evil spirits that caused illness. The light of the moon can certainly chase away fear, which can be, to those who feel it, a very "evil spirit" and fear can make us very ill. His name means Traveller, and in a meditation, He has said "I protect those who travel by night." So surely does the moonlight dispel the shadows where wrong-doers might hide.

Khonsu can inspire great love, even among those who do not usually worship the gods in their Egyptian aspects. A young priest of a Celtic tradition chose "Khensu-ka," as his Craft name. ("Khensu" is another pronunciation of the gods' name, and "ka" can be roughly translated as "double," or "spirit.") The priest knew nothing of the God except that he was drawn to Him, and wished to bear His name.

You'll sometimes see him portrayed as a hawk, wearing his moon crown. He was often connected with Horus, son of Aset and Asar. Both are divine children, and both are shown holding the crook and flail of royalty. In what seems incongruous, considering what we know of Him, Khonsu is also portrayed in mummy wrappings, just as we usually see Osiris. Why should a god who symbolizes beginnings be wrapped in the raiment of death?

For those of us in the Craft, death is not an end, it is a change, it is also a beginning. The dead are also the unborn, and birth is a

beginning. The mummy wrapping can also signify freedom from
the restrictions of the body. It must stay—you are free to go...and
begin again.

KHNUM

Hear the sound of the potter's wheel
As it spins
Khnum!

Perhaps the Smith Gods of other pantheons are more impressive, but I'm very fond of this God portrayed as a flat-horned ram; this gentle potter who forms our bodies on His wheel. The wheel spins, and firm pressure forms the blob of clay there into the seed that will become a body. The spirit enters and we begin another incarnation.

Lest you believe that my fondness for the Divine Potter denotes a reluctance to undergo the purification under the smith's hammer, let me remind you that before the clay is ever formed, it is pounded, again and again, purities removed and air bubbles smashed. You cannot make light of the heat found in a kiln, either.

When we called Him in meditation by chanting His Name, the "um" sound it became the sound of His wheel, spinning. The first thing I saw in this meditation was the top of the wheel, and on it, what I believed was the Earth. Huge hands came into my sight and began to manipulate the sphere on the wheel. As I watched, a human body formed there. The Tamerans believed Khnum created the Gods, created the Cosmic Egg from which all came, and, of course, creates the bodies in which we live. In a way, He creates our bodies by creating another egg—that which he forms on the wheel is placed in the mother's womb, there to grow in its "natural" course.

You might say that what He creates is the combination of chromosomes that will result in your body, among other things.

This God does not desert us once the egg is planted. With the Goddess Hekat, He assists at our births.

He does not create our spirits, our "selves," only the vessel in which we will live for this lifetime. If that vessel is broken, or destroyed, He feels regret, but will take the shards and rework them into new creations.

He knows that these vessels are temporary, and does not mourn at their destruction. That which is held in the vessel is eternal, so He spins the wheel, and begins to form new bodies for us, and for others.

You can pray to Khnum when you desire a child, and/or pray for a healthy one. I daresay if you yourself are a potter, you could ask Him for guidance and help in your work, too, but don't forget Ptah!

While the vessel that's tossed aside
Will return to the potter's wheel
As it spins

SESHAT

For many years, I bore this Lady's name (I hope to Her honor) as my Craft name. Her name means "She who writes." She is known as the "Lady of Literature and Libraries." She is also Goddess of Architecture, and Record-Keeping. Some refer to Her as the wife of Tehuti, an attribution that feels very right and makes perfect sense to me.

In Tameran, Her name is written "S-sh-t." We don't know the vowels. For that reason, Her name can be "Seshat," "Sashet," "Sasheeta," and so forth. I've seen it many ways.

She is also known as "Sefket," which means seven, and Her symbol includes a 7-pointed flower. She is portrayed with pen (or brush) in hand, and wearing the skin of a panther.

Even after much meditation, I'm not sure what all her symbols mean. The presence of both pen and animal skin are a source of puzzlement to me. I hope that further work will reveal at least a hint of the meaning.

Her Presence gives a feeling of vitality. She's bright, and wordy. Naturally, She's very concerned with words, and I've found that, in ritual, the things She says usually deal with words or writing. She's fussed at one member of our group for keeping his words to himself, and not sharing their beauty with others. She chided another for being too hesitant to speak.

Seshat is more concerned with record keeping than creative writing. Speak to Her when you wish to phrase something precisely rather than lyrically. Speak to Her when you want to design a house. Speak to Her when you are researching.

Better yet, let Her speak to you!

His name means "becoming," "formation," "creation," and His symbol is probably well-known to you. It is the scarab beetle.

Scarabeus sacer is a dung beetle that lays its eggs in the middle of dung which it then rolls into a ball. This ball is rolled into a hole and buried. When the eggs hatch, the dung supplies food for the little scarabs.

The Tamerans saw only that life came from defecation—they saw a miracle.

The scarab rolling the ball reminded the ancients of the sun rolling along the sky, and took the scarab also as a symbol of the sun.

Scarabs are also said to represent eternal life. From dead discarded matter came the little beetles. From death comes life. The scarab can remind us of that never-ending cycle. My own scarab is a ring, combining the scarab with a circle, another symbol of eternity and cycles.

The God symbolized by the beetle is not easy to build a personal relationship with. He is not beginnings, he is potential, formation, becoming. Yet He is not uncaring. All of us are in the process of becoming. We are hopefully becoming better, more perfect. We are striving to become one with the Lord and Lady.

Call upon Khephera when you need to remember that the Sun shines even when our half of the world is dark. For our coven, Khephera is the Sun at night, most especially at midnight. We cannot, at that time, see the Sun to show us that the day has begun, but the day has begun all the same.

Call upon this Lord when you need direction, when you want to accomplish something and are not sure how to begin...or even if you should begin. It is Khephera who will help you transform yourself, if that is your desire.

If you would know this God, go out on a dark night and meditate on the invisible Sun. Consider all the light that is hidden in the world, all the hidden energies. And know that the Sun will surely return.

HERU SA ASET
(Horus)

Hawk of Heaven, Heru!

Child of Aset and Asar, conceived after Asar's death, Heru has many aspects. He is pictured as a youth with his finger to his lips, as a hawk wearing the double crown, and as a man with a hawk's head.

More than one deity was symbolized by the hawk, and I have no trouble understanding why.

I live on a hill overlooking the San Fernando Valley. One of the delights of living here is the variety of birds we didn't see when we lived in the valley. Instead of pigeons and sparrows, we see quail, roadrunners, mockingbirds, ravens, owls, and, of course, hawks. The majority of them are red-tails, but now and then we see a glimpse of a kestrel and hear that little hawk proclaiming its own majesty.

My desk is near the patio door and I can look out over the valley. Many times, I've totally lost track of my work because I glanced out and saw a hawk, hovering in place, or soaring across the sky. I swear by all that's holy I saw one perform a chandelle (a flying stunt usually performed only by airplanes) twice! I have witnesses!

I've been known to pull over to the side of the road to watch hawks. There is something about their beauty and power that enchants me. I call to them with my love, and sing "Heru!" hoping they'll hear and know my feelings. I am exulted in that presence and lifted away from the mundane world. I long to soar with the hawks. I thirst for their freedom, their strength, their speed, their vision. Oh, yes, it is very easy for me to see in the hawk an image of the God.

Both the peregrine falcon and the kestrel bear eye-markings which are said to be the source of the well known symbol, the Eye of Horus, used not only as a symbol of Heru, but as a protective symbol as well. Hawks have incredible eyesight, and can spot a mouse running through a field from hundreds of feet in the sky. When a hawk dives feet first to capture its prey, it can go at speeds of more than 30 miles an hour.

Are you feeling sorry for the mouse? Am I going to have to give my lecture on predators again? I won't do it—I've done so at length in the section on Aset. Predators are a part of life. You are a predator. Many of the world's most magnificent animals are predators. One of the reasons I feed the various sparrows and finches that live in my area is the hope that they'll provide food for the hawks and owls. If you don't like that, I'm sorry. If you've ever communed with a hawk, I don't think you'd care what they eat.

Heru is the God most easily reached because He symbolizes the deity within. As the child of the God and Goddess, he represents each of us. If you ever have trouble contacting any deity, start with Heru, become the hawk, and soar to the heavens. From there, it is a simple matter to reach other Gods.

Heru is also known as the Avenger, referring to the battle he fought with Set to revenge his father's death and reclaim his father's throne. (The harvested grain springs anew.)

For us He represents the dawn, and the spring, both new suns.

I often speak of God/desses who are impersonal, i.e., not so much interested in the temporary, this-lifetime you as in the eternal you. Heru is not one of these. He is a very personal God. How much more personal can you get than a God who is you?

Do you wish to know this Lord? Then look inside your own heart and find the hawk that soars in the vast spaces that are inside you. Find the hawk, find the glory that He is, and you will find the glory that you are.

This Goddess' name means "mother," and the hieroglyph used both for Her name and the generic "mother" is a vulture. Many of the Mother Goddesses wear vulture headdresses.

Does that make any sense to you? I was disturbed and confused by the relationship between vultures and mothers for a long time but thanks to the help of a High Priestess in our community, Joanna, I think I understand now. In a class she was giving on the magical aspects of birds, she discussed the vulture, and the light went on over my head.

A vulture deals with corpses, with death. Mothers deal with birth. How can these go together?

Let's think of the vulture on a physical level. It eats corpses, and cleans up the landscape. All scavengers do that, of course. Some of those corpses are rotting and bloated, full of disease, a breeding ground for botulism. From the dead, poisoned flesh, the vulture takes life. A vulture can feed her children with this meat, safely.

From death, a vulture produces life, for him or her, or its young.

The Goddess, our Great Mother, is the Giver of Life and the Bringer-in of Death. Death is not an end; it is as much a beginning as birth. When you die, you leave behind something for which you have no further use. However well it has served you, that vessel is not your essence. The essential you is eternal, no matter how many times you incarnate, no matter how your body dies, no matter what happens to your body after you leave it. You could not continue to grow spiritually if you were stuck in that body after it died.

The death of the body, however, is called "the lesser death," because it is easy compared to the death of the personality. Your personality, who you are in this life, is a lot more difficult to give that up than your body. It will be extremely hard for me to give up being Ellen, for many reasons. I have so much I want to do! I know in my mind that I can accomplish just as much without being Ellen, maybe more, but I want to do it this time around. (Besides, I rather like who Ellen is and it's taken me years to get to that point. I'd like to enjoy that a while longer.)

The vulture disposes of your physical body, and serves as a symbol for the death of your personality. Until that personality is gone, you are locked up in it as surely as you had been in your physical body. And both are restrictions. Free of your physical body, you are no longer bound to the Earth. You no longer need walk to get from one place to another. You no longer need to find words to express your thoughts to another. Freed from your personality, you are no longer restricted to the knowledge of this life alone. You will know who you have been in all your lives. You can then consider all you've learned this life, rest, commune with loved ones, and, when the time is right, return to an incarnation, ready to learn more. You return to what we know as life.

Thus, Mut, and her symbol the vulture, represents the full cycle of life, not simply the cycle from birth to death as we experience it in one lifetime. She is the Goddess of all life's aspects, including death and rebirth.

If you can understand this, you can come to know this wonderful Lady.

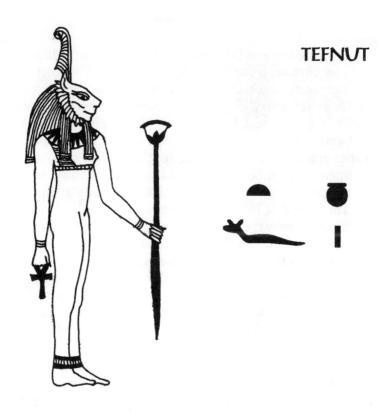

She is depicted as a lioness, and represents the moisture in the air. In our country, that could include rain. What does a lioness have to do with any of that?

I believe lions symbolized power in Tamera, and in a desert land, moisture of any sort would be very important, and therefore powerful.

I first came to know this Lady last year, when there was a forest fire within view of our house. You would be surprised what you can do when you can see the fire headed toward your home! We called on every deity, demigod/dess and mythological figure we could think of, including Tefnut. I beseeched Her to bring her moisture to the fire, to make the trees harder to burn.

No, it didn't start to rain within moments of my prayer; however, when the fire was under control, it was announced that the fire-fighter's efforts were aided by "fortuitous wind changes and unexpected moisture in the air." "Fortuitous," my Aunt Fanny! Every Witch in the San Fernando Valley was turning those winds and call

Shu and Tefnut

ing moisture! Oh, they'll never believe we had anything to do with
it, but who cares?

Of all the Tameran deities, Tefnut is the most difficult to "translate" to our culture. In fact, when we called Her to our circle, She
said just that.

"You must decide who and what I am," She said.

We've worked with that idea, and have decided who and what
She is, to us. She is the moisture in the air, the rain, the dew, the fog,
the clouds. She is perhaps more to us than She was to the Tamerans.

This Lady was usually portrayed as a human figure with the
head of a lioness. She wears an ostrich feather as does her brother
Shu.

Our first change in symbolism was to do away with the lioness-
head. Whatever the lion may have meant to the ancients, in our
minds it is inextricably connected with Fire. When we picture Her,
we see Her as a woman. The ostrich feather She wears, in our
minds, is blue.

Does the idea of deciding who and what a deity is, and choosing
the symbols to be used strike you as strange? It shouldn't. It's
exactly what happened in the first place—we've done it throughout history. The names, forms and symbols were given to the Gods
by humankind. The Lord and Lady exist without those things, and
have no need of those things. By connecting names, forms and symbols to a specific aspect of deity, we are able to narrow down our
view to that specific aspect rather than trying to deal with the
unknowable vastness that is Deity.

I can see Tefnut now, from my window. She is there in the bil-
lowing clouds that fill the sky, in the fog that obscures the valley
below me. The presence of the clouds and fog are a blessing after
the hot dry spell we suffered recently. The rain has washed the chok-
ing dust from the leaves, cleaned the air, cooled us.

However green it may look, the Los Angeles basin is desert,
made green by imported water. Only at times like this is the land
cooled, its thirst quenched by Nature.

I can feel the growing things breathing around me, their roots
drawing water and food from the moist, soft earth, and I add my
thanks to theirs as I see and feel the presence of Tefnut.

If you would honor Her, then honor the moisture in your breath, honor your own sweat, your own saliva ("tef" means "saliva"), as well as the rain, the clouds, the dew.

I have never written an entire song for this beautiful Lady. I have only one line, and upon occasion I sing it to myself. Perhaps one day I'll finish it—or perhaps you will.

Gent - le in the air and fall - ing cool up - on my skin

TANENT

The only reference I've ever found to this Lady was in Budge's *Egyptian Hieroglyphic Dictionary*, where She is said to be "a primal earth goddess."

She is indeed primal earth, but She is no personal nurturing mother, however. Tanent is more like the Grandmother of Grandmothers. She is the earth's core, the continents, the deepest sea bottom. She loves us, but in a distant way.

When you walk on the beach, digging your toes into the sand, you enjoy that beach as a whole, but are not too concerned with specific grains of sand. If one washes out to sea, you are not concerned; you know that nothing is destroyed, only changed, and the beach remains. This is the same sort of love Tanent has for us as individuals. She knows where every grain of sand is, and knows when it is washed out to sea, for She holds evens the seas in Her arms.

Yet there is more about this Lady that we found fascinating. We had done a contact ritual on Her, and at the next Moon rite, invoked Her into the Priestess. She spoke to one woman of a rock the woman had known as a child, a large rock, flat but at an angle. There, the Goddess said, the woman as a girl would go when she needed strength and peace. The woman confirmed that she had known such a rock, and had felt the Goddess there.

"I know this Lady," she exclaimed. "I always called Her the Lady of the Fields."

The presence of this Goddess was naturally very heavy, as if one's body were rooted down to the core of the earth. I found it interesting that this same description had been given to me with regard to the presence of the Irish Goddess Tara. Also attending our ritual that night was a Celtic High Priestess. She too recognized the particular "feel" of this Lady from her own practices.

All goddesses are aspects of the One Goddess, but what defines a particular aspect?—a type of energy, a purpose, a specific type of work, a "feel." Each aspect is different, and all part of the Goddess.

It would seem that the people of Tamera reached out to a specific aspect, knew Her, loved Her, and called Her "Tanent." It would also seem that the people of the British Isles reached out to the same aspect, knew Her, loved Her, and called Her "Danu."

In order to confirm our findings, we reversed the situation. In a ritual soon after, we invoked Danu. The woman who had know Tanent as "the Lady of the Fields" was present, and I knew by the look on her face we'd proven our point. The moment Danu was present, we all knew Her. It was our beloved Tanent.

"Primal Earth Goddess" in Egypt, "Mother of the Gods," in Celtic tradition—this is a very special Lady. If She did not receive ample honor in Tamera, She certainly has since in other lands, and rightly so.

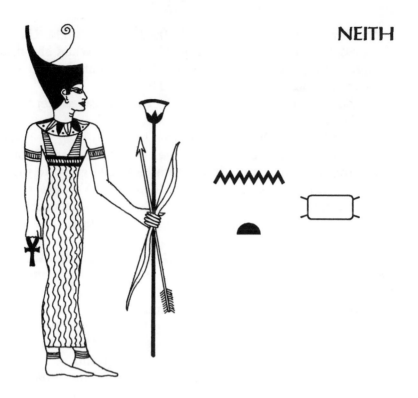

This very ancient goddess is also known as Net. She is both War Goddess and Goddess of Weaving. If you are a student of Greco-Roman mythology, this combination may sound familiar to you. The Goddess Athena had the same attributes.

As I pointed out in the discussion of Ptah, the Tamerans often reversed words to reverse meanings. The sound of Neith reversed is *"theen."* I can accept that it might be coincidence, but it does make you wonder, doesn't it?

If you would honor Neith as the ancients did, light oil lamps and candles in every corner of your house, and allow them to burn. The oil should contain some salt. I do not know the significance of this, but according to Herodotus, this is what the Tamerans did.

Neith was often credited with conceiving Herself. As a Goddess of both War and Weaving, She displays both the power of building up and breaking down. Perhaps the balance implied in the possession of both those powers implied both male and female abilities.

We contain hormones of both sexes in our own bodies. We contain both God and Goddess within. This mighty Lady displays the qualities of both, of the two sides of the coin, of the hidden and the visible.

Her symbol is variously referred to as a weaving shuttle and as a shield with crossed arrows, again reflecting Her two sides.

She symbolizes for me, as so many do, the natural cycles. Building up and breaking down both have their proper times. At the proper time, Neith is a weaver, and at others, a warrior.

If you would know Her, think on Her two symbols, on her two areas of influence. Think on times in your own past when it was right to build up, and on those times when it was right to break down. Give acceptance and honor to both types of situation.

Honor the male and female within you. In that way, you will honor Her.

OTHER EGYPTIAN GODS

Forgotten are the Gods
in lands They called their own.
Where once a hundred lived
They call one God alone.

But in our hearts They are alive,
And ever shall They be.
Oh, Ancient Ones of Egypt,
We have not forsaken Thee!

The Gods and Goddesses discussed so far are only a few of the many names and faces the Tamerans gave to the Lord and Lady. Not only were there many more, but many times the attributes of two Gods were joined together and worshipped under a combination name, e.g. Amen-Ra. I must say this went a little far at times—Ptah-Seker-Ra and similar names are only confusing to me. I find it much better to stick with the individual deities.

The list following gives brief information on other deities not discussed so far, and the glyphs for their names. Exploration of and learning about all of Them could be a lifetime's work, and though I am willing to give that time, this book would never have been finished! We continue to work with these deities and will, by the time you read this, have discovered even more about Them.

With the methods I've given you, and others you may wish to use, you can contact and learn of these deities, make them a part of you, a part of your life and work. I'd be delighted if you'd share any information you gain with our coven.

AABIT
A Singing Goddess

AAH
A Moon God

AKER

An Earth God who is shown either as two heads or two lions facing in opposite directions (east and west). You may all upon him if you are bitten by a snake, for He is said to absorb that poison from your body.

AMEN

One of the best known of the Tameran Gods, often combined with Ra. His name means "hidden," and He is the unseen qualities of the Sun; while Ra represents the qualities we can sense, light and heat. Amen is represented by a ram, was husband to Mut, and father to Khonsu.

If you are wondering why he is not discussed more fully, I can only answer that I have not felt moved to work with him to any great extent. What work we have done has shown him to be distant, not easily made personal.

AMI
A Fire God

AMI NETER
A Singing God.

AMI PE
A Lion God.

AMUTNEN
Goddess of Milk Cows.

AMU
Dawn God.

APIT
Mother Goddess,
nursing mother.

APUAT
(Also Upuat)

We have done very little work with Apuat, but what we have done has proved interesting. He is called "the opener of the ways," and is depicted exactly as Anubis is with one exception—he is white or gray instead of black. The city dedicated to Him was called "Lycopolis," "City of the Wolf," by the Greeks. He seems to be the one who, after the weighing of hearts and judgment of your soul, guides you to the place of rest. At the right time, he helps choose the way you will travel in your next life. The words that came to me were "He is both before and after Anubis."

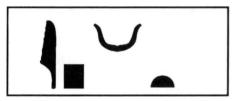

APUT
Messenger God.

ASBIT
Fire Goddess.

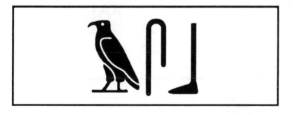

ASEB
Fire God.

ASHKIT
Goddess of the Winds.

ASHU
Water God.

AUA
God of Gifts.

AUIT
Goddess of Nurses
and Children.

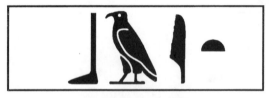

BAIT
Goddess of the Soul.

BAKET
A Hawk Goddess.

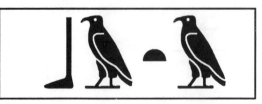

BATA
God of War and the
Chase.

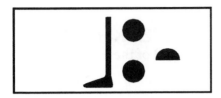

BEKHKHIT
Goddess of Dawn's Light

HAPI

God of the Nile, God of Fertility, pictured as a man with a woman's breasts. He was called "Lord of the fishes and the birds of the marshes."

HEH

God of Infinity. When he appeared on monuments and jewelry, he represented a wish that the recipient live for thousands of years.

HEKAT
(Heqet)

Goddess of Childbirth, and Protection. Her name translates as "Mistress of Magic." References to her are found as early as the pyramids. She was symbolized by a frog. With the exception of the frog, does any of this sound familiar?

HENKHESES
God of the East Wind

HESA
Singing God.

HU
The God of Taste.

HUTCHAI
God of the West Wind.

IMHOTEP

An architect and sage who was deified because of his skill and wisdom.

KEKUI (or Keku)

The God of the hour before dawn, "Bringer-in of the light."

KEKUIT

The Goddess of the hour after sunset, "Bringer-in of the night." I've done a little work with this Lady, just as it became night. The feeling I got from Her was, "Hush. Be still. You've worked hard. It is time to rest." I felt myself enfolded in soft dark gray wings.

KHURAB
A Bird Goddess.

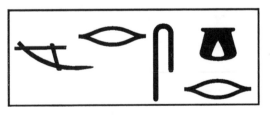

MERSEGER

"She who loves silence," a Cobra Goddess said to live on a specific mountain in Tamera.

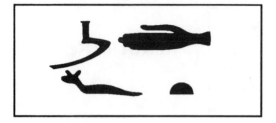

MAFDET
A Lynx Goddess.

MAHES
A Lion God.

MATHIT

Tree Goddess whose special purpose was to help the deceased climb into heaven.

MESEN
A Blacksmith God.

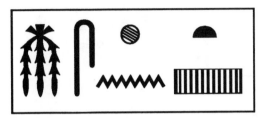 **MESKHENET**

The Goddess who presides at childbirth, symbolized by a birth brick. A woman squatted on two bricks to give birth. This may seem undignified, but no more so than the position used today which is designed for the convenience of the doctor. The ancient position used gravity to help the birth. The modern one forces the woman to fight against it.

 **MAA**
The God of Sight.

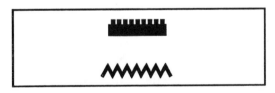 **MIN**

The God of sexual procreativity. Bees are sacred to Him. Flowers can be offered to him to stimulate fruitfulness, and "long lettuce" (lactuca sativa) was supposed to help him procreate.

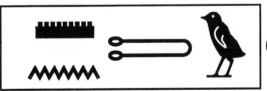 **MONTU**
(Monthu, Menthu)

War God, falcon-headed, also represented by a griffin.

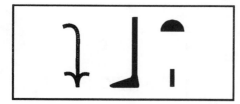

NEKHEBET
Vulture Goddess of Southern
Egypt.

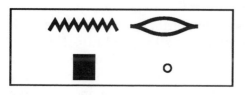

NEPER

God of grain and the prosperity of the barley and emmer wheat crops.

NERIT
Goddess of Strength.

NU
The Primal Water.

NUN
God of the Primal Ocean.

PAKHIT
A Cat Goddess.

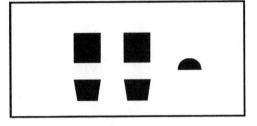

PAPAIT
Goddess of Birth.

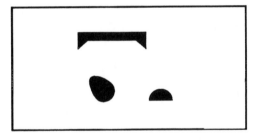

PESTIT
Goddess of
Sunrise.

PESTU
God of Light.

REKHIT
Goddess of Knowledge
Personified.

REMI
A Fish God.

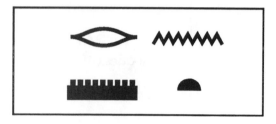

REMNIT
A Cow Goddess.

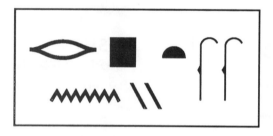

RENPITI
A God of Time.

RENENUTET

Goddess of the Harvest, depicted as a cobra. Her festivals were held at the end of planting season, and at the beginning of the harvest. She is also one of the deities said to be present at childbirth, and the one who decides how long the child will live.

SAA
The God of Touch.

SETEM
The God of Hearing.

SIA
This God personifies the
Perceptive Mind.

SHAI
A God of Destiny.
Each of us has our own
Shai, our own personal
destiny.

SHESMU
A God of Wine.

SOBEK
A benevolent Crocodile
God, also Sebek.

TAIT
A Goddess of Weaving.

TAURET
Symbolized by the
hippopotamus, She was a
protector of women
in childbirth.

TUM
Also Atum, Nefertum, and
Tem. Symbolized by the
Lotus. The Setting Sun.

UADJET
Cobra Goddess of
Northern Egypt, her name
means "Green One."

UN
God of Existence.

UNIT
A Star Goddess.

UNTA
A God of Light.

UNTABI
Goddess of the 27th day
of the month.

UNTI
A God of Light

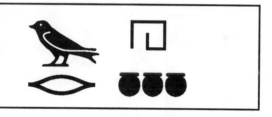

UR-HENU
A Water God.

UTCHAIT
A Goddess of the
Moon.

UTEKH
A God of Embalming.

UTET-TEFEF
God of the 29th day
of the month.

There are more, many more. I don't think I'll ever come to know Them all, but I'm going to keep trying. It is my hope that you will come to know and love many of these deities as we do. A deity only dies when forgotten, and we will not forget.

PART II

WORSHIP, RITUAL AND MEDITATION

THE CAIRO CALENDAR

The Tamerans had a calendar of 12 30-day months with five "extra" days, called the epagomenal days, occurring right before the New Year.

The year began the first day Sirius (Sothis) rose at dawn after the rising of the Nile. This took place approximately July 19 on our calendar.

Bob Brier, in his book *Ancient Egyptian Magic*, starts his version of the calendar on August 1, because Sirius now rises on approximately that date.

Since the building of the Aswan Dam, the Nile no longer floods, so the date of the inundation is a moot point.

You must decide whether you wish to go with the actual rising of Sirius, the "traditional" date, or whatever.

In the list that follows, we've started on July 19.

Most of the information that follows comes from a Papyrus called the "Cairo Calendar." The calendar contains festival notations, comments on the day, predictions and warnings. We do not understand all of the notations on the calendar, but have included them for your information and enjoyment. Further research may bring more understanding.

The comments as to whether the day is "favorable" or not come from that papyrus, as do some of the more unusual predictions and warnings. (We've reworded some of them.) Sothistar's own research and that done by members of other organizations have been added.

JULIAN DATE   TAMERAN DATE

19 July	1 Tehuti	The New Year. Celebrate. Birthday of Aten. Very favorable.
20		Anything you see will be good. Very favorable.
21	3	If you were born today, avoid crocodiles. Mostly favorable.
22	4	Stay out of boats today. In fact, stay home and do nothing. Mostly favorable.
23	5	The Gods are peaceful today. Very favorable.
24	6	If you were born today, don't take up bull-fighting or dairy farming. Mostly adverse.
25	7	Welcome the rise of the Nile. Make offerings to the Gods. What you see today will be good. Very favorable.
26	8	The day Ra goes forth. Stay home at night. Mostly favorable.

JULIAN DATE   TAMERAN DATE

27 July	9	Pacify the hearts of those on the horizon. Anything you see today will be good.
		Very favorable.
28	10	Hedj-Hotep, Goddess of Weaving, goes forth.
		Everyone is festive. If you were born today, you will die honored in old age. Very favorable.
29	11	The Great Flame (fire-spitting Cobra Goddess) goes forth. Start a fire today.
		Do not make love or look at a bull. Very unfavorable.
30	12	If you disobey Ra today, you will fall down. Stay home until sunset. Very unfavorable.
31	13	If you were born today, take care of your eyesight. Mostly unfavorable.
1 August	14	Offering to Gods in your city.
2	15	The rage of Set battles Heru. Stay out of boats. Mostly bad.

JULIAN DATE   TAMERAN DATE

3	16	Who is born today will die of a crocodile. Very unfavorable.
4	17	Festival of the Dead, Feast of the Lamps, Ceremony of Lighting the Fire, Sunset ceremony.
5	18	The day the offering to Sobek was taken away.
6	19	Chief festival of Thoth Burn incense. Eat honey and figs. Chant "Sweet is truth." Festival of Heaven and Ra. Very favorable.
7	20	The followers of Set and Ra battle. Do not work today. Very favorable.
8	21	Offerings to followers of Ra. Avoid bulls. Very favorable.
9	22	Don't eat fish or birds Don't warm oil. Very adverse.
10	23	The enemies of Ra shall suffer. Meditation and instrumental music are good, but avoid singing and dancing. Mostly negative.
11	24	The winds are peaceful for Ra's sailing. Very good.

JULIAN DATE   TAMERAN DATE

12	25	Going forth of Sekhmet to repel Set. Do not practice.
		Stay home. Mostly good.
13	26	Offerings to Asar or Tehuti.
		Transition of Aset to Het Heret head. Battle of Heru and Set. Do nothing.
		Adverse.
14	27	Peace between Heru and Set.
		Make today a holiday. Don't kill reptiles. Very favorable.
15	28	The Gods see the Children of Nut and are happy. Anything you see today will be good.
		Very good.
16	29	Don't kindle fire in the house today. Don't burn incense. Stay home at night. Mostly good.
17	30	Ritual in the House of Ra, House of Heru, House of Asar. Very good.
18	1 Ptah	The Gods are festive. The heir is established. A very good day.

JULIAN DATE   TAMERAN DATE

19	2	Ritual & Procession of Her-ur. It is important to make offerings to all the Gods.
20	3	Tehuti in presence of Ra in inaccessible shrine Tehuti orders healing of Heru's Eye. What you see today will be good. Extremely favorable.
21	4	Anpu goes forth. Anyone born today will die of a skin rash. Mostly bad.
22	5	Feast of Montu. All things performed in divine presence.Offering in presence of Hedj-Hotep. Those born today are likely to die while making love. Avoid leaving the house today. Awful!
23	6	Aset discovers She is pregnant. Plant barley, anoint with water, egg & milk. Those born today should avoid drinking.Wonderful.
24	7	Ra kills the Children of Rebellion. Any born today will die in foreign lands. Do nothing today. Terrible
25	8	Whatever you see today is good. A great day.

JULIAN DATE	TAMERAN DATE	
26	9	Jubilation in the heart of Ra. All enemies are destroyed. If you were born today you will live to a ripe old age. Very favorable.
27	10	Procession of Bast and ritual. A good day.
28	11	Today the front piece of the-prow is fixed on the Sacred Boat. Property and life are before the August One. All is good. Very favorable.
29	12	Terrible.
30	13	Satisfy the hearts of the Great Gods. Feast. Very favorable.
31	14	Receiving the White Crown of Heru. Offerings to local Gods and pacify spirits.
1 September	15	Ra and his followers go out at night. Don't look Don't leave your house Mostly adverse.
2	16	Feast of Asar Unnefer. All His followers rejoice. Everything you see today will be good.

JULIAN DATE TAMERAN DATE

3	17	The earliest Gods come forth from the waters of Nun. It is important to make offerings of bread and beer and to burn incense. Very favorable.
4	18	Anpu ritual of Transformation. Do nothing. Not good at all.
5	19	Nun goes forth to set up the djed-pillar. Very good.
6	20	Ra makes an example of the rebels, overseen by Tehuti. A bad day.
7	21	Going forth of Neith. Her eyes guide Tehuti. Mostly bad.
8	22	Do not bathe today. Bad, bad, bad.
9	23	Birthday of the Staff of the Sun. If you were born today, stay away from crocodiles. Bad.
10	24	If the wind is blowing, do not go out of your house until after sunset. Worse.
11	25	The Children of Rebellion are found in a burial mat. Do not go on any road today. Very adverse.

JULIAN DATE   TAMERAN DATE

12	26	The windows at the palace of Business are opened and sealed. Don't lay the foundation of a house or put a ship in a shipyard. Don't work at all. Very bad.
13	27	Don't go out. Don't work until the sun sets. If you will born today, avoid snakes. A bad day.
14	28	Whatever you see today will be good. Very favorable.
15	29	If you are born today, you will die honored among your people. A wonderful day.
16	30	Land in festivity. Festival of Ra. Festival of Asar and Heru. Very favorable.
17	1 Het Heret	Feast of Het Heret. Very favorable.
18	2	Wedjoyet returns from Dep.
19	3	If you see anything on this day it will be good.
20	4	The earth trembles under Nun today. If you value your house, don't navigate today. Terrible.

JULIAN DATE   TAMERAN DATE

21	5	The day of the blaming by His Majesty of this God. Very adverse.
22	6	Ritual of the Gods of the Two Lands. Very favorable. What you see today will be good. A good day.
24	8	Today Aset goes forth pleased because Her Son is granted His heritage.
25	9	This is the day of the Blaming of the Great Ones. Do not go outside. Do not let light fall on your face until Ra sets. Adverse.
26	10	There is rejoicing in Heaven. Ra's crew is at peace. Those in the fields are working. Very favorable.
27	11	You will see good things today. Very good.
28	12	Pacification of the hearts of the Gods, wherever they are. Once more the Udjat Eye is in the head of Ra.
29	13	Asar sails upstream to Abydos. Very adverse.

JULIAN DATE   TAMERAN DATE

30	14	Set's actions cause grief in the hearts of the Gods. Do nothing. Bad.
1 October	15	Day of the inspecting of Ba-Neb-Dedet, God of Sexual Fertility. Adverse.
2	16	Appearance of the eight gods of Ashmuneium. A happy day of in eternity and infinity. A favorable day.
3	17	Landing of the Great Ones at Abydos. Aset and Nebet Het weep over the death of Asar. Very bad.
4	18	This is a day of strife for the Children of Geb. Do not begin a journey.
5	19	The day of the children of the storm. Do not sail or navigate a boat today.
6	20	Bast goes forth angry Anyone born today may catch the plague. A terrible day.
7	21	The Feast of Shu. Very Favorable.
8	22	The day of the raising of the statue of Maat.

JULIAN DATE	TAMERAN DATE	
9	23	Today Ra judges. Adverse.
10	24	Aset goes forth happy as does Nebet Het. They have Seen Asar and he has given his throne to Heru. Very good.
11	25	Whatever you see today will please the hearts of the Gods. Good.
12	26	Establishing the tet pillar of Atum. Egypt is given to Heru and the desert to Set. Tehuti judges before Ra.
13	27	The day of judging of Set and Heru. The Lords are satisfied causing the doors to open. Very favorable.
14	28	A day of festival: Decree establishes Heru as King. The Gods rejoice. Very good.
15	29	The three noble ladies of the Tan-nenet go to the presence of Ptah and praise Ra. The white crown is given to Heru and the red to Set. Favorable.
16	30	Day of the House of Ra and Asar. All you see today will be good. Very good

JULIAN DATE   TAMERAN DATE

17	1 Sekhmet	Ra is joyful in his beauty. The Gods rejoice. A good day.
18	2	God/desses, Heaven and Land in festivity. Whatever you see today will be good. Favorable.
19	3	Do not do anything today. Anyone born on this day will die of his ears. Not a good day.
20	4	Perform rituals of Sebek in his temple and in your house. This will please the Gods. A very good day.
21	5	Het Heret goes forth in the presence of the Great Ones at Kher Aba. Life, stability and welfare are given to Her. Favorable.
22	6	The barque of Ra is established to overthrow the enemies immediately. Stay home. Very adverse.
23	7	Very adverse.
24	8	Very favorable. Whatever you see will be good.

JULIAN DATE   TAMERAN DATE

25	9	Ra speaks, Tehuti acts. Very favorable.
26	10	Anyone born today will die in old age as beer enters his mouth. Very favorable.
27	11	Feast of Asar at Abydos. The unborn are joyful. Wonderful.
28	12	Day of transformation into the Bennu. Offer to your Bennu in your house. Do not go out in the wind. Bad.
29	13	Holiday in your house. Going forth of Het Heret, who is pleased in the presence of Ra. The Gods rejoice.
30	14	Two Goddesses of Weaving; Hedj-hotep and Tayet go forth to hand their things over to Neith. A good day.
31	15	Feast of Sekhmet and Bast
1 November	16	Papyrus damaged.
2	17	People and Gods judge speech of crew of Heliopolis when Heru arrives. Do not go out at midday. A bad day

JULIAN DATE   TAMERAN DATE

3	18	The boat of the God is over-thrown. Terrible.
4	19	The day of making ointment for Asar. Do not taste bread or beer. Drink only grape juice until sun sets.
5	20	The day of looking at the sun disk. Do not go out. Do not anoint yourself. Not good.
6	21	Setting up the tet pillar.
7	22	Festival of ploughing the Earth. Placing of the Hennu boat. You will see good things today. Mostly favorable.
8	23	Do not go out at night. If you see a lion it will kill you. But the day is mostly favorable.
9	24	Papyrus damaged.
10	25	Papyrus damaged.
11	26	Favorable.
12	27	Murder of Osiris Mysteries Favorable.
13	28	Grief and search by Aset Very adverse.

JULIAN DATE   TAMERAN DATE

JULIAN DATE	TAMERAN DATE	
14	29	Finding of Asar's body. Rejoicing.
15	30	Make offerings to God/desses, invocation, offering food to spirits. A good day.
16	1 Amsu	Festival of Bast. Good.
17	2	Make a holiday in your house. Favorable.
18	3	Do not burn fire in the presence of Ra.
19	4	If you are born today, you will die old among your people. Good.
20	5	Day of Sekhmet and purifying the flame. She is violent. Mostly bad.
21	6	Double the offerings today. Favorable.
22	7	Do not make love where the Sun can see you. Bad.
23	8	You will see good things today. Very good.
24	9	Offerings to Sekhmet. Make cakes and repeat the offerings. The Gods will be pleased. Very good.

JULIAN DATE   TAMERAN DATE

25	10	The day of the coming forth of flame together with Heru form the marshes. Do not burn papyrus today. Not good.
26	11	Don't get near fire today. Very bad.
27	12	Answering every speech of Sekhmet. Do not approach any dogs today.
28	13	Day of prolonging life and making beneficial Maat in the temple. Favorable.
29	14	Aset and Nebet Het weep in remembrance of what Asar had been. Don't listen to singing or chanting. Terrible.
30	15	Nun goes forth through the cavern to where the Gods are in darkness. Anything you see today will be good. Very good.
1 December	16	The going forth of Shu. Very favorable.
2	17	Nun goes forth to the Gods. All come into existence. Do not wash yourself in water today.

JULIAN DATE	TAMERAN DATE	
3	18	Going forth of Gods to Abydos.
	19	Very adverse.
5	20	Going forth of Bast. Do nothing. Bad.
6	21	Bast guards the Two Lands Make abet offerings to followers of Ra. Great.
7	22	Anything you see will be good. Good.
8	23	If you are born today, you will die in great old age, rich in all that is good.
9	24	Happiness is on both heaven and Earth. Wonderful.
10	25	The Great Cow is established in Ra's majestic presence. Don't drink milk. Do drink and eat honey.
11	26	Do not go out until Ra sets. Very adverse.
12	27	There is great festivity in Hefau. A good day.
13	28	Tehuti takes an oath in Ashmineum. Going forth of the Noble One. Make a holiday in your house. Very good.

JULIAN DATE   TAMERAN DATE

14	29	Day of appearance of Hu Tehuti sends forth to Bast and Sekhmet to guide the Two Lands. What you see today will be good. Very good.
15	30	Crossing over in the presence of Nun in from Temple of Hapi. Offer incense to all Gods. Favorable.
16	1 Rekh-Ur	God/desses in festivity. Feast of Ptah lifting Heaven of Ra. Festival of the Little-Heat. Good.
17	2	Gods receive Ra, hearts are festive. Better.
8	3	Going forth of Set. Stay home. Horrible.
1	4	Offering to your Spirits and-local Gods. Show your heart to the Gods. Very good.
20	5	All you see today will be good. Great.
21	6	Putting up the Tet pillars of Asar. Festival of the Great Heat. Very adverse.
22	7	Invocation, offerings in your house to Spirits. Make abet offerings to the Gods.

JULIAN DATE   TAMERAN DATE

23	8	The God/desses are in festivity. Very favorable.
24	9	The God enters to distribute the ration of all the Gods. Very good.
25	10	Elevating the female Gods of the Temple. Birth of Heru-sa-Aset. Going forth of Udjat eye for singing. Awful.
26	11	Feast of Neith. Going forth of Sebek to guide Her. You will see good from Her hands. A good day.
27	12	Everything you see will be good. Favorable.
28	13	Proceeding of Sekhmet to Letopolis. Stay home. Not good.
29	14	Do not go out at dawn on this day. Most good.
30	15	The Gods go forth for Him in Heaven.
31	16	Aset is awakened by Ra. Heru saves His father.

JULIAN DATE   TAMERAN DATE

1 January	17	Day of keeping things of the Wabet of Asar which have been placed in the hands of Anpu. Very favorable.
2	18	The seven executioners go forth. Bad.
3	19	The day of the mourning of the God. Do not go out alone in the day time. Adverse.
4	20	Proceeding of Goddesses of Heaven southward. Very adverse.
5	21	The day of the birth of cattle.
6	22	Festival of Ptah and Heru. Anything you see today will be good. Very favorable day.
7	23	Festival of Aset. Everything you see will be good today. Great day.
8	24	Festival of Aset. Birth of Aion. Do not approach rivers today. Not great.
9	25	All you see today is good Good day.
10	26	Going forth of Min to Coptos. Aset sees Min's face and joins Him.

JULIAN DATE	TAMERAN DATE	
11	27	Feast of Seker.
12	28	Unnefer is pleased. The unborn rejoice. Wonderful.
13	29	There is uproar among the Children of Geb. Do nothing. Very bad.
14	30	Talk to no one. Very adverse.
15	1 Amenhotep	Feast of entering into Heaven and two banks. Entry of Asar into the Moon. Heru rejoices. Great.
16	2	Everything you see is good. Super day.
17	3	Papyrus damaged.
18	4	Set calls to battle. Bad.
19	5	Neith goes forth from Sais, when they see her beauty in the night for 4 1/2 hours. Do not go out during this time. Favorable.
20	6	Jubilation of Asar in Busiris. Going forth of Anpu. Make ritual. Very favorable.
21	7	Followers of Ra called to Heaven. Do not leave your house until Ra sets. Very adverse.

JULIAN DATE   TAMERAN DATE

22	8	Making the way for the Gods of Khnum. All you see is good. Good day.
23	9	The Day of Judgment in Heliopolis. Very favorable.
24	10	Coming of Tehuti. Very adverse.
25	11	Very favorable. Bad.
26	12	The day the Nile comes from Nun. Give food. Great.
27	13	Day Tehuti and Spirits go forth. Any ritual performed will be good. Wonderful.
28	14	Day of making health. Stay home. Awful.
29	15	Day of rebellion in the shrine. Don't work.
30	16	Day of opening of the doorways and court at Karnak. Don't look at anything in the darkness today. Very adverse.
31	17	Do not pronounce the name of Set today or you will fight eternally in your house. Bad.
1 February	18	Feast of Nut, She who counts the days. Make a holiday.

JULIAN DATE	TAMERAN DATE	
2	19	Day of the birth of Nut anew. Stay home and don't look into the light.
3	20	Do not leave the house. Do not look into the light. Very bad.
4	21	Omitted by scribal error.
5	22	Birth of Apophis. Do not think of pronouncing the names of the snakes. Obviously very adverse.
6	23	Feast of Heru in Kemwer. Very good.
7	24	Do not leave the house. Very bad.
8	25	Do nothing today.
9	26	The day He is sent into the cave without knowledge of the Great Ones to look for the occasion of coming. Bad.
10	27	Do nothing today. Very bad.
11	28	Feast of Asar at Abydos. Very good.
12	29	Anything you see will be good.

JULIAN DATE   TAMERAN DATE

13	30	The Feast in Busiris.
14	1 Rennutet	The enemies are struck. there is a great feast in Heaven. Very favorable.
15	2	Geb goes to throne of Busiris to see Anpu who commands the council to learn the requirements of the day. Very favorable.
16	3	The day the Great Ones and the Uraeus fought. Any lion who pronounces the name of the constellation Orion will die immediately. Do nothing. Very bad.
17	4	The Gods and Goddesses are satisfied when they see the Children of Geb. Whatever you see today will be good. Very favorable.
18	5	Hero is well when the Red One sees His form. Whoever approaches today will find anger.
19	6	The stars go forth bitterly and openly. Whoever sees small cattle today will die at once. Bad.
20	7	Going forth of Min into the festival tent. Put myrrh on the fire.

JULIAN DATE   TAMERAN DATE

21	8	Day all the parts of the Eyes of Heru are accounted for Excellent.
22	9	Do not go out into the darkness. Terrible.
23	10	The Great Ones are introduced to the whole eye of Heru. All you see today will be good.
24	11	Very adverse.
25	12	Very adverse.
26	13	Asar is conducted to his ship at Abydos. Very bad.
27	14	Do not be courageous today. Very adverse.
28	15	It is a happy day in Heaven. Very favorable.
1 March	16	Going forth of Kephera. Every town is joyful. Great.
2	17	Going forth of Set. Adverse.
3	18	Do not approach in the morning. Do not bathe with water today. Very bad.
4	19	Feasting in Heliopolis. Ra goes forth in his bark across Heaven. All you see today will be good. Positive.

JULIAN DATE	TAMERAN DATE	
5	20	Today Ra repels those who rebel against their masters. Do not work today. Bad.
6	21	Do not go out today. Extremely adverse.
7	22	Very adverse.
8	23	The day of making offerings to the Spirits at Abydos. Bad.
9	24	Set rebels against Unnefer. Do not mention the name of Set today, or you will have strife in your house forever. Very bad.
10	25	The day of cutting out the tongue of Sobek. Do not eat anything which is on the water. Very bad.
11	26	Papyrus damaged.
12	27	End of the world by Sekhmet. Do not go out until Ra sets. Terrible.
13	28	What you see today will be good. Very favorable.
14	29	Adoration to Unnefer. Offer local Gods myrhh on fire. Very good.
15	30	Offerings to all Gods. Offerings to Ra, Asar, Horus. Very favorable.

JULIAN DATE   TAMERAN DATE

16	1 Khonsu	Feast of Heru-sa-Aset and followers.
17	2	Do not sail today. Bad.
18	3	You will see good things today. Very good.
19	4	Do not leave the house. Follow Heru today. Bad.
20	5	Feast of Ba-neb-dedet, God of Sexual Fertility. Very bad.
21	6	Coming of the Great Ones of the House of Ra. Festival of reconstituting the heavens. Festival of Aset. All you see today will be good. Great.
22	7	Every heart is glad. Every land is happy. Wonderful.
23	8	What you see today is good.
24	9	Same as yesterday.
25	10	The White One of Heaven proceeds downstream. Adverse.
26	11	Papyrus damaged.
27	12	Adverse.
28	13	Papyrus damaged.

JULIAN DATE   TAMERAN DATE

29	14	Very adverse.
30	15	Papyrus damaged.
31	16	Do not leave your house until sunset. Bad.
1 April	17	All you see today will be good. Very good.
2	18	A time of rejoicing among the Gods. What you see today is good. Very favorable.
3	19	Day of counting by Tehuti who heard Maat. All Gods rejoice. Great.
4	20	Maat judges. Very adverse.
5	21	Very adverse.
6	22	Anyone born this day will live to be very old. Very favorable.
7	23	Everything you see today will be good. Very good.
8	24	Papyrus damaged.
9	25	Papyrus damaged.
10	26	You'll see good things today. Favorable.
1	27	Very adverse.

JULIAN DATE	TAMERAN DATE	
12	28	All you see today is good. Good.
13	29	Papyrus damaged.
14	30	House of Ra, House of Asar, House of Heru. Excellent.
15	1 Heru	Festival of Heru. Festival of Bast. Great.
16	2	Hearts of the Gods. Listen Very well. Holiday of Ra and followers.
17	3	The day is fixed as a feast on both Heaven and Earth. Good.
18	4	Geb and Nut are judged by the Gods. Don't shout at any being today. Adverse.
19	5	You'll see good things. Good.
20	6	Heru avenges His father.
21	7	Feast of Udject: festival, singing, chant. Adverse.
22	8	Make a holiday for Ra and His followers. Make this day a good one. Favorable.
23	9	Make incense of various sweet herbs for Ra's followers. Very good.

JULIAN DATE   TAMERAN DATE

24	10	Anyone born today will be noble. Great.
25	11	The followers of Ra catch birds and fish. Avoid sailing on the river. Bad.
26	12	You will see only good. Great day.
27	13	The Feast of the Udjat. Singing, chanting, and offerings of incense and sweet herbs.
28	14	What you see today will be good. Wonderful.
29	15	The day of fighting. Do not judge yourself this day. Very bad.
30	16	Anyone born today will become a magistrate. Good.
1 May	17	Stay home. The worst.
2	18	Asar goes forth from His house to the august mountain. Don't eat lion meat today.
3	19	The Ennead sails repeatedly not good.
4	20	The day many will die if an adverse wind comes. Bad.

JULIAN DATE	TAMERAN DATE	
5	21	The day of the living children of Nut. Do not go out before dawn.
6	22	Shu complains to Ra about the Great Ones of Infinity. Stay home. Bad.
7	23	The crew rests when it sees the enemy of its master. Good.
8	24	What you see today shall be good. Very good.
9	25	Everyone is pacified by the sun disk. Very favorable.
10	26	Going forth of Neith. Very adverse.
11	27	There is an uproar among the Gods. Do not work. Adverse.
12	28	Day of purifying things. Festival today. Do not go against events. Very good.
13	29	What you see today will be good. Very favorable.
14	30	Going forth of Shu. Appearance of Tehuti. Very good.
15	1 Uatchet	Great Feast of the Southern Heavens. Festival of Bast. Feast of Het Heret. Wonderful.

JULIAN DATE   TAMERAN DATE

JULIAN DATE	TAMERAN DATE	
16	2	Every God/dess spends the day in festival and great awe in the Sacred Temple. Very favourable.
17	3	The anger of the Divine Majesty. Do nothing. Very adverse.
18	4	Whatever you see today will be good. Very good.
19	5	Het Heret departs. The Gods are sad. Stay home. Stay away from boats. Stay away from work. Very bad.
20	6	All the Goddess's temples are in an uproar. Do not make an uproar in your house. Very bad.
21	7	Sailing of the Gods after the Goddess. Bad.
22	8	The massacre of the followers of the Goddess. Do not beat anyone. Very adverse.
23	9	The Gods are content. Every God is in festivity. Very good.
24	10	The day of creating enmity, the hearts of the Gods are sad. Bad.

JULIAN DATE   TAMERAN DATE

JULIAN DATE	TAMERAN DATE	
25	11	The Great Ones learn what Ra saw through the eyes of Her Ur. Do not perform any ritual. Bad.
26	12	Reception of Ra, holiday and festival. Very good.
27	13	Ra sails westward to see the beauty of Unnefer. Bad.
28	14	Maat and Ra go forth in secret. Stay home. Very bad.
29	15	Heru hears your words in the presence of all Gods and Goddesses. Good things will be seen in your house. Very good.
30	16	Day of transporting Maat to the Shrine of Ra. Adverse.
31	17	The escape of the Fugitive Eye. Bad.
1 June	18	Maat and Ra go forth in secret.
2	19	Very adverse.
3	20	Stay home today. Very adverse.
4	21	What you see will be good. Mostly good.

JULIAN DATE   TAMERAN DATE

5	22	The day of Sepa of Tura. Do not look at any digging, skin rash, or fever today. Adverse.
6	23	The day of quarrelling with Unnefer. Bad.
7	24	The day of the Children of Bedesh. The God kills them when He comes, then sails south. Very favorable.
8	25	The Great Enemy is in the Temple of Sekhmet. Don't go out at midday. Mostly good.
9	26	What you see today will be good. Favorable.
10	27	The day of sailing down the river and tearing down the enclosure wall. Stay home. Very bad.
11	28	The day of creating misery. Very bad.
12	29	Festival of Mut. Feeding of the Gods and Mut's followers. Very good.
13	30	Ceremony of Heru-Merti Very favorable.

JULIAN DATE	TAMERAN DATE	
14	1 Heru-Khuiti	Send abet offerings. All Gods and Goddess feast. Very good.
15	2	Maat and all Gods perform rites as One Who is in Heaven. Very good.
16	3	Feast of the Goddess of Heliopolis. Stay home. Bad.
17	4	Procession of Sopdu and youthful followers. Mostly bad.
18	5	Temple is festive. Min is at Akhmin What you see will be good. Very good.
19	6	The day of transporting Unnefer to Rostau. Do nothing. Very bad.
		Very bad.
20	7	The Dead One arrives on Earth. Whoever approaches Him will be trampled by a bull. Very adverse.
21	8	Utchat ceremony. Anpu ceremony. Favorable.
22	9	If you are born this day, you will have noble honor. Very favorable.

JULIAN DATE	TAMERAN DATE	
23	10	The day the Eye of Ra enters. Very good.
24	11	Destructiveness is created in the presence of the followers of Ra. Bad.
25	12	Day of jubilation throughout the land. Very good.
26	13	Holiday for Heru followers, defenders of the Son.
27	14	Very good.
28	15	Ra goes forth to propritiate Nun. Very bad.
29	16	Pour ritual water for those in your next world. Very good.
30	17	You'll see good things. Good.
1 July	18	The crew leads the rebels. Stay home in the morning. Bad.
2	19	The Eye of Heru returns. Feast of your local god. Appease your spirit. Very good.
3	20	Cleansing and renewal of the Noble Ones. Very adverse.

JULIAN DATE   TAMERAN DATE

4	21	What you see will be good. Very favorable.
5	22	Feast of Anpu. Followers of Geb and Nut in festivity. Purification of the Gods. Very good.
6	23	Do not taste bread or beer on this day. Very bad.
7	24	Abet offerings to gods in presence of Ra. Holiday in your house. Very good.
8	25	The God is established. Very favorable.
9	26	The Gods sail. Do not go out at noon. Mostly good.
10	27	Do nothing. Very bad.
11	28	Feast of Min. Very good.
12	29	Holiday in Temple of Seker. Very favorable.
13	30	Birthday of Ra. Any rite good today. Sing and make offerings. Very favorable.
14	1	Birthday of Asar. Very Favorable.
15	2	Birthday of Her Ur. Very favorable.

JULIAN DATE   TAMERAN DATE

16	3	Birthday of Set. Very favorable.
17	4	Birthday of Aset. Very favorable.
18	5	Birthday of Nebt Het. Very favorable.

RITUALS

What little we have found in the way of rituals as performed by the Tamerans shows these rites were very different from Wiccan ceremonies. We have, of course, very detailed records of the funeral ceremonies, but even if we wish to perform a crossing-over rite, these would not be suitable in most situations. These rituals do have some use for us in life, but that is discussed later in the book.

There were indeed celebrations of many kinds in Tamera, as you see by the calendar. We don't know many details about these, but I seriously doubt they were circle ceremonies. None of this is unexpected. They were not Witches. They had their own religion, in fact several of them.

As I have said, Sothistar is not trying to recreate the ancient Egyptian religion. We are a Wicca coven, and we work with the Tameran Gods. The rituals you will find here are written with that mindset.

Although these rituals and their various elements are certainly designed so that you may use them "as is," I urge you to add as many personal touches as you wish. It is more important that the rituals touch you than that you do them exactly as I have written.

These rituals were written especially for this book, and although they may contain elements found in Sothistar's rituals, and /or may have been performed by our coven, they are not necessarily traditional with us. If we performed these rites, we would add our own touches to make them uniquely Sothistar's, just as I hope you will.

Below you will find a Circle Opening and a Circle closing to be used with the two rituals. You may, of course, use them with other rituals if you like.

Circle Opening

All gather at the place of the ritual. If the individual or group have a special Circle Opening for calling the elements, etc., it may be performed before this opening. Using a wand, staff, or athame, draw the symbol of the throne to the East, saying:

> *The Lady Aset stands before me.*

Turn to the West, and draw there the hieroglyph for Nebet Het, saying:

> *The Lady Nebet Het behind me.*

Turn to the North, draw there the eye and the throne for Asar, saying:

> *To my left, my Lord Asar.*

Turn to the South, and draw there the hawk or the face which signifies Heru, saying:

> *To my right, my Lord Heru.*

Again face East, and make a sweeping motion with your head from the Eastern edge of the circle to the Western edge, saying:

> *Nut above me.*

Make another sweeping motion from West to East, but this time with the wand lowered, saying:

> *Geb below me.*

Face East again, and say:

> *Safe I stand within the Gods*
> *Blessed be the work done within this sphere.*

Proceed with the ritual.

Circle Closing

Begin at the East and as you mention each deity's name, turn in that direction, and bow.

> *Our work is ended. We thank the Lady Aset, Lord Heru, the Lady Nebet Het, Lord Asar, Lady Nut and Lord Geb for their protection and guidance.*
>
> *Although we shall leave our formal circle, we ask that the love, protection and guidance we have received from these deities continue, for we shall ever be in need of those blessings.*

If you have a formal Circle Closing, it may be done now. If not, rap on the altar and say:

The rite is ended.

CELEBRATION OF THE BIRTHDAY
OF THE GODS

For many years, Sothistar held a "Birthday of the God/dess" party to celebrate the birth of five Egyptian deities. I am unaware of any traditional birthdates for deities of other pantheons, so we celebrated the birthdays of all the Gods and Goddesses of all pantheons at this party.

These celebrations were held on the Saturday or Sunday that fell within the five days preceding July 19, the date of the rising of Sirius. This ritual celebrates the births of the five deities, but is designed so that you may add names in order to celebrate Gods of all pantheons, if you wish.

A participant should be chosen to represent each of the five deities. All others in the circle should be given (or choose) the name of other deities of the Egyptian pantheon (or any pantheon).

To add to the spirit of the celebration, this ritual can (and should be) followed by a pot-luck feast. Information on traditional foods can be found in Part III.

Circle is opened.

Priest: *My friends, we are gathered here to celebrate, with joy and love, the birthday of five worshipped in an ancient land.*

Priestess: *Five they were, born of the Sky, fathered by the Earth. Five they were, born one each day in the five days not of the year.*

Priest: *Five were born of the Sky Mother—three sons and two daughters. Let us first honor Them, one by one.*

Priestess goes to the participant representing Asar, bows and says:

> *Praise to Thee, Asar, eldest son of Nut. God of Life, Lord of Death, Ruler of the Unborn. Receive Thee our love and adoration as we celebrate the day of Your birth.*

159

Asar: *First born of Our Mother am I, first to see the land, first to
           call it beloved. I am the grain that must fall if life is to be
           renewed. It is my voice you hear in the last sigh of earth and
           the first cry of birth. If you would honor me, then honor all
           phases of life including its end, for I am both, and I shall be
           with you when your life begins and when it ceases.*

Priest goes to the one representing Aset, bows and says:

           *All love to Thee, Aset, Lady of the Moon, Daughter of the
           Sky. Mother, Mistress of all Magic, our hearts rejoice at Your
           presence on the day of Your birth.*

Aset: *I am Our Mother's first daughter—the fullness of the Moon
           am I. I am the brightness of learning. Magic is mine, and
           power. I am all that is Woman, all its strengths and all its
           burdens. If you would honor me, honor all my children. Serve
           them, and you will serve me.*

Priestess goes to one chosen to represent Heru, bows and says:

           *Her Ur, Thou Great Sky, Thou Great Face, honor and praise
           we bring to Thee. Lord of all, hear our joy as we celebrate the
           time of thy birth.*

Heru: *I am the sky beyond the sky, watching all, seeing all through
           the Sun and the Moon. Little known am I, but that does not
           limit my power. If you would honor me, then honor your-
           selves, for all creation is mine.*

Priest goes to one chosen to represent Nebet Het, bows and says:

           *Beautiful Nebet Het, Lady of the House, Lady of the Womb, happily
           do we praise Thee. Know Thou of our love as we celebrate your birth.*

Nebet Het: *All that is unseen am I—all that is unknown. Mystery is
           mine, and meditation. Do not seek to know me—I will come
           when I choose, and when you least expect me. If you would
           honor me, honor that which you do not know, nor understand.*

Priestess goes to one chosen to represent Set, bows and says:

> *Hail, Mighty Set! Sword wielder, storm bringer, reaper of the grain. Hear us, hear our praise as we honor the season of your birth.*

Set: *I am the desert storm, wind-scouring, sand-blasting. I cleanse, but not gently. Those who do not understand see me as evil, for they do not see that I give by cutting away. If you would honor me, then honor your eternal selves, for that is what I honor in my work.*

Priest and Priestess return to their original positions. Priestess takes up the chalice, saying:

> *The Mother of these Gods, the Womb from which They came forth, was the Goddess of the Sky, the Lady Nut. We cannot honor Them, without honoring Her. Partake of the cup, taking within you the Mother of the Gods, rejoicing in the joy and pain of birth.*

Priestess raises the chalice in a salute, sips from it, and passes it to the Priest who follows suit, and passes the chalice on.

When that chalice has returned, the Priest takes up the bread, saying:

> *Nor can we celebrate this birth without honoring the Father of the Gods, Geb, Lord of the Earth. Partake of the bread, honoring this Great God, rejoicing in the strength and beauty of His seed.*

Priest raises the bread, takes a small piece and eats it. He then passes the plate to the next person.

When the bread has returned, the Priestess says:

All Gods are one God, all Goddesses are one Goddess. Let us now, in that spirit, call out the other names by which our Lord and Lady are known, with love and praise, that we may, as much as possible, honor the whole.

She calls out a name and the others follow suit around the circle. It will be most effective if, after you've gone around the circle once, you do it again, several times. If, instead of calling out the names, each person sings the name, in whatever notes they choose, you will find it quite lovely and moving.

Priest: *Hail to the Lord and Lady by all Their Names!*

Priestess *Let us now close our circle and continue our celebration with feasting and laughter, remembering as we do that this is as much a part of our celebration as this ritual.*

Circle is closed.

THE RITE OF BLESSING A CHILD

Before the rite, the parents should, with careful thought, choose a deity to serve as protector of the child, and prepare a child's amulet as detailed on page 208. A small cloth or leather bag to hold the amulet should also be prepared.

If possible, one person should be chosen to represent each of the Gods who bring a gift to the child. If enough people are not available, those present can rotate.

If desired, each of the gifts given in the name of the deities during the right can be symbolized by an actual gift to be placed in a small bag or box. Suggestions can be found at the end of each speech. Most of the deities mentioned in this right are traditionally connected with childbirth.

Circle is opened.

Priestess: *We are gathered to celebrate a joyous event—a loved one has returned to us.*

Priest: *A soul has entrusted itself and its upbringing to two of our members.* (To parents) *Bring the child forth.*

Parents step forward with child to stand facing Priest and Priestess.

Priestess: *It is not our right to choose the path our children will follow. That choice belongs to each individual. When this child has reached the age of decision, he/she will choose the way of the spirit that is right for him/her.*

Priest: *Until that time, however, we can direct our children along the path we have chosen. And we can place that them under the protection of the Gods as we know and love Them.*

Priestess: *Before the Gods, name this child.*

      (Done)

Priest: *As we rejoice in this returning of a loved one, let us bring to this small one the gifts of the Gods.*

Parents may stand in the center of the circle, each person stepping forward to bestow a gift, or the child may be carried around the circle. If symbols of the gifts are presented, they should be given to the parent not holding the child.

Priest: *The Lord Asar has sent forth* (child's name) *from the Land of the Unborn. But He sends no spirit forth alone. In the name of the Father of all, do I bring the gift of guidance throughout life* (a small compass).

Priestess: *In the name of Aset, Birth-giver, do I give the gift of love, that this small spirit may both love and be loved in return.* (a small heart)

Khnum: *From Khnum who created the seed for the body of this child, do I bright the gift of health* (a tiny pot, or chip of baked clay).

Heqet: *In the name of Heqet, Mistress of Magic, midwife, do I bring power and fertility of mind* (a small frog charm).

Bes: *Bes, God of Joy and Protection, brings the gift of humor, of joy, of healing laughter* (a small item of silliness).

Meskhnet: *In the name of She who is the foundation on which birth takes place, I bring a foundation on which this child may stand firm throughout life* (a tiny chip of brick).

Anpu: *Anpu, Guardian of Souls, gives the ability to see the truth* (a small candle).

Priest: *What deity have you chosen to protect this child?*

Parents name the deity. Amulet is brought forth and held toward center of circle. If a God has been chosen, Priestess reads the following; if Goddess, the Priest. The other will read the words of the amulet.

Priest/ess: (deity name,) *let your power enter this amulet. Let the words written here be Your words, let their truth be Your truth, and the voice which speaks the words be heard by all as Your voice.*

Priest/ess reads amulet.

All envision the power of the deity entering the amulet. The name of the God or Goddess may be chanted or sung, or a song may be inserted here.

The amulet and a small symbol of the deity shall be placed in the bag which is placed around the child's neck.

If godparents have been chosen, they should be called forth at this time.

Priestess: *Before the Gods, will you, (Goddessmother,) take upon yourself for this child's spiritual upbringing, and if need should come, for his/her physical well-being, as though he/she were born from your womb?*

Goddessmother responds.

Priest: *Before the Gods, will you, (Godfather,) take upon yourself for this child's spiritual upbringing, and if need should come, for his/her physical well- being, as though he/she were grew from your seed?*

Godfather responds. The Godparents step back into the circle. Mother now comes before altar and prays in these words, or words of her own choosing.

My Lady Aset, Mother of All, Mistress of Magic, help me to raise my child with love and wisdom, leading him/her in the right ways. Be ever by my side that I may be the mother to my son/daughter you are to me.

Father steps forward and prays in these words, or words of his own choosing.

My Lord Asar, Father of all, Lord of Life and Death, into my hands you have given this child. Guide me that I may guide her/him to full growth. Strengthen me that I may ever be a source of strength to her/him. Be ever at my side that I may be the father to my son/daughter you are to me.

Priestess: (Mother,) *what vows will you make to this child, who, though he/she comes to you in this small body, may have carried you in her/his arms in another life.*

Mother makes vows.

Priest: (Father,) *what vows do you make to this small spirit who may be even older and wiser that any here?*

Father makes vows.

Priestess: *This child, born to our brother and sister, is now under the protection of the Gods. Can we do less? Let us each promise our love and protection to this small one.*

Child is carried around circle as each member makes promise.

Priest: *May we always be worthy of the trust the (Gods) ave placed in us. Our work is done.*

Circle is closed.

RITUAL OF TRANSFORMATION

This rite is one written by Ember as part of her required coven work. It can be done as part of a Moon Rite. Because of its nature, it would most properly be done at New Moon (dark of the moon). Although it is written for a group to perform, it makes a lovely solitary rite as well.

The transformation sought in this ritual is not instant transformation or revelation, but the slow transformation of the natural cycles of birth, death, decay, and rebirth. Do not expect the transformation wrought, as Ember put it, by "flash floods and forest fires." The results of this ritual will be slow and steady. Most spiritual growth is not instantaneous. In this rite, you seek to begin transformation, just as the planting of the seed can one day result in a tall tree.

Materials needed:

For each attending:

One votive candle

A small flower pot two-thirds filled with potting soil, and a saucer.

A large seed or small bulb (i.e. avocado, onion, garlic clove, large nut—anything that will grow).

Piece of paper.

Writing instrument.

A scarab or drawing of a scarab.

A pitcher of water should be available.

If, of course, your elemental attributions are not those we use, feel free to rearrange the elemental invocations to suit your tradition.

Circle is opened.

As the following invocations are made, concentrate on the power we all have to transform ourselves, and on the powers outside ourselves that can assist our work.

At the East:

> *Lords and Ladies of the East, Powers of Air, be welcome in our circle. Your power is the transforming power of intelligence, the power to blow away cobwebs and let in the light. Lift us on Your wings, that we may see and understand the insight you would bring us. Blessed be.*

At the South:

> *Lords and Ladies of the South, Powers of Fire, be welcome in ourcircle. Teach us your transforming power, the slow burn of nitrogen, the heat of elemental reactions. Warm our hearts and strengthen our courage, that we may bring about the changes we desire. Blessed be.*

At the West:

> *Lords and Ladies of the West, Powers of Water, be welcome in our circle. From you life first came forth upon the world; lend us the fecundity of the sea, to conceive and nurture the changes we desire. Blessed be.*

At the North:

> *Lords and Ladies of the North, Powers of Earth, be welcome in our circle. Powers of Death and Life, and of the*

*slow changes of rock and tree, teach us patience and deter-
mination, to foster the growth we work for. Blessed be.*

At the center (or wherever your main altar is):

*Great Isis, you bring forth life from death, birth from still-
ness. Let us, who would learn from Thee, bring about
growth from pain, hope from despair, change from stag-
nation. We honor you in our meeting and celebration;
help us to honor you in our lives as we grow toward you.
Blessed be.*

*Osiris, Lord of Life and Death, you are the educator of
your people in life, as well as after it. Teach us what we
need to know, to make the changes which will bring us
ever closer to you.*

The scarab should now be placed in the center of the circle where
all can see it as Khephera is invoked. As the words are spoken,
think on the symbolism of the scarab in hieroglyphs: It means "to
transform, to begin, to become."

*Oh, Thou, who workest change in darkness and hidden
places, grace our circle with your presence; grace our lives
with transformation. As, through you, the sun is born out
of darkness, may our spirits be enlightened through our
own pain and our own shadows. Teach us to know thee
and learn from thy ways.*

All now concentrate on the scarabs they hold. If desired, Khephera's name may be chanted or sung. We find that if all will sing
out a name in whatever notes or rhythm they feel appropriate, it is
an effective and moving invocation.

Just as in a contact ritual, all should concentrate on the presence of
the God, calling Him in their hearts and asking for His presence.
When each feels the presence, he or she should cease to chant and
"listen" to the God.

When all have ended their communion with the Lord, thanks should be given to the God for his presence and his wisdom. If you like, all may speak of their meditations and what they learned. (If not now, it is a good idea to do so after the ritual.)

All now take a piece of paper and write upon it that which they wish to transform. All take seeds and wrap the paper around them, placing them in the pots. The pitcher of water is passed so that the seeds may be watered.

Circle Leader says:

> *As the seed swells and grows in darkness, so will that which you wish to transform. In honor now, of the light born in darkness, and knowing that as the moon, unseen, grows toward full so does the work we have planted tonight, let us bring light to our own circle.*

Each person takes a votive. The Circle Leader begins by lighting his or her own, and hands it to the person to the left, with a wish or a prayer for his or her life. That person lights the candle he or she was holding, and passes it to the next, and so on around the circle.

When all are holding burning votives, the Gods and Elements are thanked.

Circle is closed.

All should take their candles and pots home.

RITE FOR CHARGING A USHABTI FIGURE

The figure should be complete, although, if you wish, you may add a few finishing touches during the ritual. Before you begin, think carefully of the purpose of the figure. As an example, this ritual is written for a figure that will help seek out a magical family, i.e. a coven or magical group.

Circle is opened.

Stand in the center of your circle and say:

> *Here stand I, alone but for the presence of the Gods. I would stand in the presence of those who are of kindred spirit, who love the Gods as I do. I come to this circle to ask the help of the Gods and the powers of the elements in my search for those who would be my family.*

Take the figure and go to the East, and say:

> *Lady Aset, Lovely Winged One, I present this figure. Know that it is an extension of my self and my will. I ask your blessings upon it, and upon me, that you might aid my search to find those of Your children who would join me in my love and worship of You.*

Turn to the West, and say:

> *Nebet Het, Beautiful Lady of Mystery, I present this figure. Know that it is an extension of my self and my will. I ask Your blessings upon it, and upon me, so that which is hidden from me may be made known, and I may find those with whom I can share bonds of love.*

Turn to the North, and say:

*My Lord Asar, Lord of Life and Death, I present this fig-
ure. Know that it is an extension of my self and my will.
I ask Your blessings upon it, and upon me, that it may
share my life forces, and help me to find those with whom
I may walk in your path.*

Turn to the South and say:

*Mighty Heru, Lord of the Sun, I present this figure.
Know that it is an extension of my self and my will. I ask
Your blessings upon it, and upon me, that this figure may
gain the sight of the hawk, to seek out those with whom I
would work and worship.*

Pass the figure through the smoke of incense, saying:

*By the Powers of Air, do I share my breath, that you may
do the work for which I have created you as part of myself.*

Pass the figure through the flame of a candle, saying:

*By the Powers of Fire, do I share the warmth of my body,
that you may do the work for which I have created you as
part of myself.*

Sprinkle the figure with water, saying:

*By the Powers of Water, do I share with you my blood, that
you may do the work for which I have created you as part
of myself.*

Sprinkle the figure with salt, saying:

*By the Powers of Earth, do I share with you the strength
of my body, that you may do the work for which I have
created you as part of myself.*

Raise the figure on high, saying:

> *Behold, thou art* (your name,) *Begin now the work*
> *which is your purpose in being. When your work is done*
> *your powers will return to me.*

Circle is closed.

MEDITATIONS

CONTACT RITUALS

We refer to these as "rituals" but they are, in truth, somewhere between a ritual and a meditation. They are deliberately very simple in order that concentration is on the deity to be contacted. Please note, however, that although they seem passive, they are not. The work being done is not expressed physically or verbally for the most part, but it is still work, and it is still being done.

You do not need any equipment for this rite, but those who are new to this type of work may find it helpful to have a picture, statue or symbol of the deity you are contacting. For example, we recently did a contact ritual on Shu, the Egyptian God of the Air. We used a small center altar on which we placed a yellow candle (yellow symbolizes Air for us), sandalwood incense (incense also symbolizes Air, and sandalwood is a clean fresh fragrance), and a yellow ostrich feather, (Shu is portrayed wearing an ostrich feather). It helped, too, that we were having 60 mile an hour winds that night, but such special effects aren't necessary.

We usually perform contact rituals sitting down. Often, instead of sitting in a circle, we find a comfortable place about the living room, and cast the circle around the room. We find it more important to be comfortable than formal for this work.

Use the simplest circle casting possible. If you like, you can recite the following, visualizing a circle of white light forming around you:

> Circle, now we conjure thee
> That thou mayest a boundary be
> Between the world of men we know
> And what the Mighty Ones shall show.

A guardian and protection be
For power we shall raise in thee.
Preserve, contain it in thy sphere
To aid the work we shall do here.
So have we consecrated thee.
So may our circle blessed be.

If you wish to invoke the elements, again, keep it simple. If you've used the poem above, and wish to continue in this vein, use the following:

Sky and sun and sea and earth,
Teach us, give our wisdom birth.
Sun and sea and earth and sky,
With your powers gather nigh.
Sea and earth and sky and sun,
All together four and one.
Earth and sky and sun and sea,
Join us as we call to thee.

Feel free to rearrange this to suit your own quarter system.

At this time, you may ask the Lord and Lady to be present. I recommend that you do not use names here, that is, do not call Aset and Asar, for example, or any particular name, because you do not want to turn minds toward any deity name but that which is the subject of your ritual. Lord and Lady, God and Goddess—these are fine.

Loving Lady, Mighty Lord,
By cup and shield and wand and sword,
We ask your presence and your light
To bless the work we do this night.

Once this is done, the work of the ritual begins. You may discuss what you know of the deity, any legends of which you are aware. Begin visualizing the deity in the middle of the circle, putting as much energy and concentration into the visualization as you are able. What you are doing is building a telesmic image, building a form suitable for the deity to enter.

At the same time, you might find it helpful to chant the name, or, if you have one (and there are several later on in the book), sing an appropriate song. We often us a "bell" chant, also known as a free-form chant. Each person sings the name of the deity as each feels it, whatever note or notes seem right. This is very effective, and almost always lovely.

When you feel the presence of the deity, stop chanting. At this point, mentally ask the deity what He or She would have you know. Listen for the answer in your head. When you feel you have an answer, you may ask other questions. Some deities will "take over" and give you more information without your asking. (Oh, for a psychic tape recorder!) Someone observing such a ritual would see all in the circle sitting quietly, and would not realize that there is more here than blanking out and waiting for the deity to show up and say something. It is important that all involved have worked at the visualization and called the God or Goddess to come and teach.

If this is performed by a group, the leader should wait until all have finished their visit with the God or Goddess. When all have finished, thank the deity for what you've learned, and close the circle. Make notes, or share your experiences with each other. This is the most important part of the ritual. You will find, often, that although each individual has had a personal experience, there will be a thread of similarity running through those experiences.

Pay attention to events of the next several days, for it often happens that things regarding this deity may crop up.

Don't worry if the information you've received does not match what the historians and Egyptologists have told us. We are interested in what the Gods tell us, who They are now, how They relate to us, now, here.

Done properly, these rituals can have a very strong effect on the participants. The deity will become real, become a part of each person, rather than a distant, unknowable being. The love I have always felt for Asar is nothing compared to the adoration I feel for Him after I met Him in a contact ritual.

Do not feel you must accept and understand every bit of information you receive. Make note of it, research it, work with it, and wait to see what comes later. You will learn what is truth and what isn't. It is also valuable to do more than one contact ritual on a specific deity, with a space of time between. As you grow, the deities will have more and different things to teach you.

If you will use this ritual/meditation method, you will learn immeasurable amounts about the Gods, and gain a personal knowledge of Them you might not have imagined possible.

GUIDED MEDITATIONS

The following meditations are introductions to some of the Tameran deities. We usually use them with people who are new to our coven, but will sometimes repeat them for students who have been with us a while. As is true of the contact rituals, these help build personal relationships with the deities introduced, or further those relationships. If nothing else, they are relaxing and enjoyable.

Chris and I have found it best to read these together. If the deity is male, I read the narration and he reads the words of the deity; if female, he reads the narration, and I, the spoken words.

All should make themselves comfortable. The room should be darkened as much as possible, leaving only as much light as is necessary for the leader (or leaders) to read the meditation.

We have found it most effective to have a relaxation period in which the students are mentally led away from the every day world and problems. Below are both a "leading away" and a "leading back. "These (or something else if you have something you like better) are to be read at the beginning and the end of each meditation.

After the meditation, those involved should describe their experiences and feelings. We do, of course, allow them to keep silent if the experience was too personal to share. This seldom happens in a close group, however.

Many groups in our area use similar meditations based on their own pantheons. Whatever your tradition, you'll find this type of work valuable.

Beginning:

Close your eyes. Make yourself as comfortable as possible. Breathe slowly, and evenly. IN-two-three-four. OUT-two-three-four.

Let your awareness of your body fade away. You are surrounded and held by darkness, a soft comforting darkness. You float upon it, drift upon it, drift away from tension, from worry, from problems. There is nothing but you and the darkness, the soft, nurturing, peaceful dark. *(Short pause.)*

Your body has no weight, no pain, no problems.

You are moving without effort, without intention.

You do not know where you are going, but you know it is right for you to go there. *(Short pause.)*

Your movement has stopped, and that, too, is as it should be. You feel your feet touch the ground, and you open your eyes. *Go to the guided meditation.*

Ending:

Again the darkness lifts you, cradles you, carries you away in its undemanding softness.

You know, as you move, you approach your every day life, but you find that the problems and tensions you left behind have lost their power to confound you. You know that they are temporary, that all except the gods and the essence of yourself is temporary. You know that you bear with you the power of *subject of meditation* and with that, you can conquer all. You have stopped your movement. Your body takes on weight, you become aware of your physical surroundings. This room is beginning to become visible. Take a deep breath, let it out slowly, and return to your normal state.

Asar—Pharaoh

You are standing by a river, broad and full. Tall palms grow beside it.

The sun beats down on your body, and you welcome it. It feels good, soaking into your skin, soothing muscles, warming you. Its heat, and the sounds and sights of the river bring you a feeling of peace. For the moment you are content to look, and listen, and feel.

At the edge of the river, growing from the water, are green stalks, a plant you recognize as papyrus. Amongst them stands a bird with a long curved beak. He is very still, eyes closed, and seems to be thinking deep, serious thoughts.

Out on the river, fisherman cast their nets. Their voices drift back over the water as they call to each other. Some of them are singing as they work.

Near you, a field of barley thrives. A slight breeze whispers through its leaves.

You become aware of a presence behind you—so powerful a presence that you hesitate to turn—yet you know you must, and slowly, you do.

The figure you see is tall, and strongly built. He wears a nemyss of dark blue and gold striped material—the same cloth used in His short kilt. A pectoral of lapis lazuli with a large scarab in the center stands out against His bronze chest.

His expression reveals nothing of His thoughts. Yet you feel the power of His presence, His very being—and you are overcome by it—by Him. Without meaning to move, you find yourself at His feet.

For a moment, you hear only the beating of your own heart. Then, in a voice that is firm, tinged perhaps with amusement, he says, "The pharaohs that were my image needed homage to remind them of me. I do not. Rise."

A bit dazed, you start to stand up. He reaches down to help you, and you take his hand as a child might reach to its father.

"Walk with me," He says, and you know that where He leads, you will follow.

Beside Asar, you walk between the river and the barley field. He reminds you that He taught His people the skill of agriculture, turned them from nomads into the progenitors of a great civilization.

"This is often forgotten," He muses. "Think more on my life. Your people think too much of my death."

He ponders the barley for a moment, and speaks, almost to Himself. "I tried to teach them of life and death through the grain. but they did not understand. I had to teach them through my own death." He is silent for several heartbeats—staring at the grain before Him.

Just when you think He has forgotten you, He turns back with a warming smile. "Come," He says. "Let us walk farther. I have much to tell you." And you walk beside Him, and listen.

A long pause (at least five minutes) should be made here to allow the students to experience their own time with Asar.

Finally, you stop. He turns to bid you farewell, and to give you his blessing.

You leave Him, and return to the place where you began. Slowly, the land of Egypt fades away as the familiar darkness surrounds you.

Go to ending.

Nebet Het

You have come to rest on a solid surface, but when you open your eyes, you find yourself in darkness. Although you can hear sounds around you, and feel solidity beneath your feet, you can see nothing. There is no moon to give light.

You peer into the darkness, waiting for your eyes to adjust, straining to gather in the slightest hint of light. What is here, you wonder. Is there anything here?

Out of the darkness, you hear a woman's voice.

"What do you see, child, when your eyes are closed? Nothing. Does that mean everything has disappeared?"

Again there is silence. To your left, however, you see a shadowy feminine figure, and you move toward it.

When you reach the figure, however, you discover it was a trick of the light, a swirling of shadow.

The voice comes again, from another direction. "Has the moon only one side? Because you cannot see it, does it have no existence?"

"Who are you?" you ask. And from yet another direction, you hear "I am that which is not what it seems to be."

You move toward the sound of her voice, but find nothing. "By misdirection do I lead," you hear from a distance. "As Isis is to Ra, so am I to Khephera. I am mystery."

Another shadowy figure appears ahead of you and this time you are sure it is not a trick. You move quickly toward it.

Reaching it, however, you find nothing but shadows in the darkness, and frustrated you cry out "Lady!"

The voice says, "Child, if you would seek me, seek me not, but be."

You stand where you are, trying to be patient.

Short pause of about one minute.

And finally, you feel Her Presence. You cannot see Her clearly, but She is there, and Her hand is held out to you. You take it, stand with Nebet Het, feeling the joy of Her nearness. Spend this time with Her, learning from Her. Learn what She will teach you.

Long pause.

It is time to return. Bid a loving farewell to the Goddess and close your eyes. Feel yourself surrounded by the comforting darkness.

Meditation—Tehuti

You are standing by a river, broad and full. Tall palms grow beside it.

The sun beats down on your body, and you welcome it. It feels good, soaking into your skin, soothing muscles, warming you. Its heat, and the sights and sounds of the river, bring you a feeling of peace. For the moment, you are content to look, listen, and feel.

At the edge of the water grow tall green stalks, a plant you recognize as the papyrus. Among them stands a bird with a long curved beak. He is very still, eyes closed, and seems to be thinking serious, profound thoughts.

As you watch, he opens his eyes, turns his head and looks at you, seems to study you. You are surprised to see, when you return the look, the eyes are intelligent, even wise. After a moment, the bird nods as if he has made a decision. He spreads his wings, and takes to the air. You turn to watch his flight as he passes you.

Your attention is drawn to a path over which the bird flies. You wonder where it leads, and you follow it, through the grain field.

After a few moments, you see ahead a building, made of mud brick, with windows high in the walls.

A doorway faces you, and you enter through it. You find yourself in a surprisingly bright room. On two walls are cubicles full of scrolls. The other walls are covered with murals and hiero-glyphs.

The doorway is momentarily darkened as a figure enters from the courtyard. It is a strange personage who approaches . . . the body of a man, but with the head of the bird who led you here.

Somehow, though, you do not find this strange. The eyes that look on you are full of wisdom, and you have the feeling that the knowledge in that long-beaked head is far beyond those contained in these cubicles; for this is, you realize, Tehuti, the teacher, Lord of

Wisdom, inventor of hieroglyphics, master of hidden knowledge, Lord of books and science.

Without speaking, he leads you to a table. There sit two men, each drawing on papyrus. It is possible they have the same skills, but the work you see is not of equal quality. One is drawing clean precise hieroglyphs. The other's work is rough, his papyrus stained with ink blots.

You notice that the second man's pen is blunt and crude, the papyrus not smooth. The first man has a better brush and a better papyrus. It is no wonder there is a difference in their work.

Tehuti nods as if he knows your thoughts, and says, "The proper tools are necessary."

He leads you to another scholar, a young man who is apparently just learning to scribe. He slowly and carefully draws the same pictograph over and over.

You look up to see Tehuti's eyes upon you.

He turns, motions for you to follow, and leads you out to the courtyard. The Lord shows you the plants there, the fish in the pool.

He says, "There is much I have to teach you, but there is work for you to do. There are things that you must know, knowledge you must have before I can teach you the greater mysteries. The papyrus on which I write must be fine and smooth. The brush on which I write must be well made. The ink must be finely ground and of good quality."

"All these things must be prepared by you, though the work is hard and often tedious. Prepare the tools, and you will be ready to learn what I have to teach."

Stay here a while with the Lord Most Wise. Perhaps he will have other wisdom to share with you.

It is time to leave the Lord of Wisdom. You rise and bid him a respectful farewell.

You walk back through the scrolls. . .

Out the door to the path . . . .

Through the grain to the river.

The river fades, slowly . . . slowly . . . as the darkness reappears.

Meditation—Anpu

You find yourself in darkness. Though you can see nothing, you can feel a slight breeze. It gives you a feeling of vast open space. You here small sounds in the night.

You move your feet, and learn from the feel and sound that you stand on the rock and the sand.

Your eyes are beginning to adjust to the dark. You can see sand, and mounds, and nearby, some cliffs . . dark spaces in them to indicate openings of some sort.

You realize, with no little trepidation, where you are. You are in the Valley of the Kings . . burial palace of pharaohs, of queens, of nobility. . . and you are alone.

There is a scuttling in the sand, near your feet. What is it? A scorpion, perhaps? A beetle?

What is that slithering sound over there? Perhaps a horned asp . . .or some harmless serpent.

Another sound catches your attention. You can't quite tell what it is—but it is coming nearer. . closer. The sound changes from one moment to the next. At first it seems like the step of an animal—the next moment, the measured tread of a human.

You can see something coming, but in the darkness, you cannot discern what it is . . .a man . . .or something else.

You strain to see. . .strain to hear . . try to learn what is approaching.

Before you can the figure stands before you—neither man nor animal—but both—the body of a man and the snarling black head of a jackal!

You are face to face with Anpu, Anpu the Guardian of the Tombs, Guide of the Underworld, the Challenger.

You may escape if you wish, you have only to open your physical eyes and you will be safe—away from those eyes that look deep into your soul—away from this denizen of the Underworld—away from the teeth revealed by His snarl.

What will you do? Will you open your eyes? Or face the challenge of the jackal?

If the student chooses to open his or her eyes at this point, stop. If more than one person is involved in the meditation, signal for the student

*to leave the room so you can continue. Later, reassure him or her that it is
all right . . he or she just wasn't ready.*

You stand, and after moments, Anpu ceases to snarl. He
speaks:

"I am the Challenger. Those who cannot face me are unworthy
or unready to walk the ways I guard. They shall not learn the
deeper secrets, shall not see that which is hidden.

"You have faced my challenge—you shall learn.

"Know this, I guard not only the hidden ways, but those who
travel them. If you find yourself in the dark and afraid, reach out
into the darkness, feel my hand holding yours. I will remove you
from your fear."

Anpu may have more to tell you. Stay a while in the presence
of this mighty God. Glory in His presence, for that in itself may
teach you much.

It is time to leave the Valley of the Kings and Lord Anpu. Bid
him farewell—as the Valley fades away—and a strange thing happens: for a moment, instead of black, the head of the God seems to
be golden.

The village fades away—slowly—slowly—and slowly there is
total darkness.

SONGS FOR THE GODS

What was the music like in Tamera? We know the style of music in modern Egypt, but information is limited on ancient times.

Dr. Jihad Racy, when he did the music for the Tutankhamen exhibit in Seattle, studied the ancient instruments shown in the drawings, the music still used around Egypt, and came up with what he believes is close to that music. See "Sources" for name and producer.

I am not a musician nor an historian. These songs are from my heart, in love and celebration of the Gods I love, not from any great amount of musical training or skill. The first few were born when I was giving a lecture on the Tameran Gods. I wanted to show how beautiful They were to me and to express my love for Them, in the hope that some of those listening would learn to love Them, too.

I chose to introduce Them by retelling the legend of Aset and Asar, and including, when possible, songs that introduced the deities as I knew Them, as I loved Them. In the years since, as I have come to know more and more of Them, songs have been added, beyond those deities involved in the legends.

We've used these effectively as invocations, prayers, or simple expressions of love.

Because I find it difficult to separate the legend and the songs in my mind, I include both here.

In an age long past, by a mighty river of changing colors, there was an enchanted realm. There grew the stately sycamore, the acacia, the fruitful palm, and the papyrus. There wandered the gazelle, the oryx, the hare, the lion, and the jackal. About the river, life flourished; the ibis, many kinds of fish, the crocodile, and the hippopotamus. And the sky held an abundance of winged ones, the swallow, the kite, the vulture, ducks and geese, and soaring above them all, the hawk.

This kingdom had many names, but one most vividly described the feeling of the people for their country: Ta Mera, "Beloved Land."

These people knew and loved many Gods and Goddesses, among them a beautiful Goddess of the sky whose name was Nut.

The ancients portrayed Her stretched across the heavens, with her feet to the East, and her hands to the West. The stars, they said, were jewels on her body, and the Milky Way was milk from her breasts.

Hymn to Nut

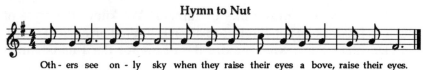

Oth - ers see   on - ly   sky   when they raise their eyes a bove, raise their eyes.

Others see
Only sky
When they raise their eyes above
Raise their eyes.

Mother Nut,
They are blind,
For they see not with their hearts
But their minds.

I can see
High above
How you cover all the world with your love.

I can see
With my heart
Thou art beautiful to see
O Thou Art.

The Lady Nut was beloved of her people, and beloved also of the Lord of the Earth, Geb, the God who can be seen in mountains thrusting up from the Earth, in the steep cliffs of a canyon, in the granite precipice. The people of Tamera saw this Lord stretched below his Lady, like Her with his feet to the East and his head to the West, and they felt his strength and vitality rising from the Earth.

Hym to Geb

Lord of the Earth and the plains and the high - est mount - ain,
Lord of the for - est and hills and the deep - est cav - ern!
Geb! We hon-or Thee. Geb! We hon-or Thee Lord of the Earth, praise to Thee.

Lord of the Earth and the plains

And the highest mountain.
Lord of the forest and hills
And the deepest cavern!
Geb! We honor Thee!
Geb! We honor Thee!

Lord of the rocks and the cliffs
And the darkest cave. Oh,
Lord of the desert and sand,
Now we sing our praise to
Geb! We honor Thee!
Geb! We honor Thee!
Lord of the Earth, praise to Thee!

Nut and Geb were lovers, and as happens when two so love, it came to pass that Nut found herself with child. What would often be an occasion for rejoicing was a potential tragedy, for though the beloved of Nut was Geb, Lord of the Earth, the husband of Nut was Ra, Lord of the Sun.

Hail Ra!

Bright - ly he shines, our gol - den one! Hail Ra! Rul - er of the sun! Ho-ly one on high, Rul - er of the sky! Let your voi - ces ring in praise of Ra, our King!

Brightly he shines, the golden one.
Hail, Ra! Ruler of the sun!

Holy one on high, Ruler of the sky.
Let your voices ring
In praise of Ra, our King.

Father in heaven, shining bright.
Hail, Ra! Bringer of the light.

Holy one on high, Ruler of the sky.
Let your voices ring
In praise of Ra, our king!

Thou who art Life, all praise to thee!
Hail, Ra! Ever blessed be!

Holy One on high, ruler of the sky!
Let your voices ring In praise of Ra, our King.

Powerful was the Sun in this ancient land, and powerful was
Ra. So powerful that when another Sun god, Amen, came to promi-
nence, the Tamerans added Ra's name to His, for none could ignore
this Mighty Lord.

In his not totally unreasonable anger, Ra pronounced a curse
upon the children carried in the womb of the Lady. The children
would not, He proclaimed, be born in any day of the year.

Our story might have ended here, were it not for yet another God, Tehuti, Lord of Words, Lord of Wisdom, inventor of hieroglyphs, the wisest mage and teacher of all time.

Wisdom Has Wings

Wis-dom has wings. Wis-dom can fly. Could wis-dom come to one such as I? Teach-er of Gods, teach-er of kings, O, I would learn from Thee I would earn wings, I would earn wings.

Wisdom has wings. Wisdom can fly.
Could wisdom come to one such as I?
    CHORUS
Teacher of gods, teacher of kings.
Oh, I would learn from thee, I would earn wings.

Head of an ibis, eyes of a mage.
Wisest of all wise ones, holiest sage.
    CHORUS

Lord, hear my cry! Feel my heart reach!
My life is learning if you will but teach!
    CHORUS

One cannot be wise without being loving, and the wise and loving Tehuti took pity on our beautiful Goddess. He played draughts with the Moon, and won one seventy-second part of each day, creating five new days in the year. During these days, Nut gave birth to three sons and two daughters; Asar, Set, Her Ur, Aset and Nebet Het.

First born, Asar, known to the Greeks as Osiris, became King of Tamera. Under His guidance, the people of Tamera learned to plant the seeds in the nurturing Earth and to reap the harvest of their labors. He taught them to care for the wild cattle and wild birds, that the food they represented would be available without a hunt. What had been a primitive people became a mighty civilization.

Osiris

O - si - ris, O - si - ris, O - si - ris, Lord.

Osiris, Osiris,
Osiris, Lord.

Pharaoh of two lands,
Hold us in your hands.
Osiris, Lord

King of Life and Death,
Fill us with your breath.
Osiris, Lord

Holy is Thy Name.
Warm us with your flame.
Osiris, Lord.

Ruler of the Nile
Touch us with your smile
Osiris, Lord.

Osiris, Osiris,
Osiris, Lord

Ruling by his side, the Lady Aset, sister, wife and Queen, Mistress of Magic, perhaps the most beautiful Goddess of all. Queen She was, and mighty in power, blinding in beauty, and loving beyond human understanding.

A Song for Aset

Seek you star-light that sings? Seek you ma-gic with wings? Would you laugh and then cry? Seek you joy? Seek you joy? Seek you love with-out end, sis-ter, Mo-ther and friend Come with me, I will show you my La-dy show you my La-dy. Come with me, I will show you my La-dy

Seek you starlight that sings?
Seek you magic with wings?
Would you laugh and then cry?
Seek you joy? Seek you joy?
Seek you love without end,
Sister, Mother and friend?
Come with me,
I will show you my Lady.

Would your spirit unfold
Gaining wisdom untold?
Would you look on a beauty
That's blinding to see?
Are there worlds you would know?
Seek you power to grow?
Come with me,
I will show you my Lady.

Beloved was Asar, beloved was Aset. But Set, Their brother, was not beloved by many of the people. They did not understand that His work, the storm, was as necessary to life as peace, and that breaking down was as much a part of nature as building up. Many did not see His Glory.

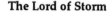

The Lord of Storm

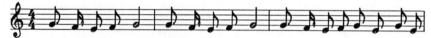

Comes the de - sert Wind! Comes the de - sert Storm! Comes the lord of all whose time is

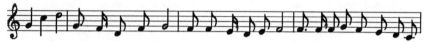

at an end! When the storm has passed, the temp'-ral will be gone. On -ly the e - ter - nal shall re-

main In His wake.

Comes the desert wind!
Comes the desert storm!
Comes the Lord of all whose time is at an end.
When the storm has passed
The temporal is gone.
Only the eternal shall remain
In His wake!

Seek you now to grow?
Seek you now to change?
Seek you to be one with all eternity?
Stand and face the winds
And when the storm is passed
Only the eternal shall remain
In His wake.

Set of the Red Hair, Lord of Storm, envied His brother the love the people bore Asar; and in his own home, Set found more reason for envy, for the eyes of his wife and sister, Nebet Het, gazed upon Asar with such love that Set became enraged.

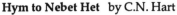

Hym to Nebet Het by C.N. Hart

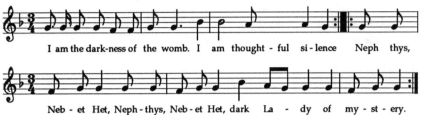

I am the darkness of the womb.
I am thoughtful silence.
I am the stillness of the tomb.
I am thoughtful silence.

CHORUS: Nephthys, Nebet Het
               Nephthys, Nebet Het
               Dark Lady of Mystery. (2x)

I am the starlight in the night.
I am thoughtful silence.
Soft the sounds of wings in flight.
I am thoughtful silence.

I am the chorus of the breeze.
I am thoughtful silence.
Whispered winds through limbs of trees.
I am thoughtful silence.

It is said, in legend, that Nebet Het and Asar were lovers. Some say the Goddess deceived the Lord by taking on the likeness of Aset. Others say Asar knew. And many say that Aset knew of the union, and in Her boundless love, blessed the joining.

A child was born to Nebet Het, a child of hidden light, Anpu, Guardian of the Underworld, Guide of Souls—Anpu, the Observer, Anpu, the Challenger.

The Challenge

Do you dare to walk the hidden ways?
Do you dare to walk the hidden ways?
Do you dare to face the Jackal?
Do you dare to face the Jackal?
Do you dare to walk the hidden ways?

Can you bear to face the hidden truth?
Can you bear to face the hidden truth?
Can you bear to face the Jackal?
Can you bear to face the Jackal?
Can you bear to face the hidden truth?

Set could bear no more, and the Lord of Storm conceived a plan. He called to His presence the craftsmen of greatest skill. To them He gave this order: Build a sarcophagus suitable for the body of a God. Build it of the finest woods, inlay it with the most precious jewels, beautify it with gold. Build it, He ordered, to the exact dimensions of the King, Asar.

When the sarcophagus was completed, Set held a banquet in Asar's honor. Music there was, and dance, and a glorious feast. When the feast was over, Set announced a contest. He revealed the glorious sarcophagus, worthy of a God, and proclaimed that whosoever fit it exactly would receive it as a gift.

One by one, those at the banquet lay down in the coffin, and one by one each rose again, for all were too tall, or too short, too thin or too fat, too narrow of shoulder or too wide of hip.

The last to enter the sarcophagus was Asar, Lord of Tamera. He had only time to discover the perfect fit when Set and His henchmen fell upon the sarcophagus, and sealed it with lead, imprisoning the King.

Together, Set and His conspirators carried the coffin out of the banquet hall. Hidden by the darkness, they took it down to the river and placed it in the water, where it floated away into the black night.

Word came to Aset of the death of Her Lord and Love, and She cried out in pain. As was the custom, She tore Her hair, rent Her garments, and mourned.

Mourning Song

Mourn, my Country, mourn,
The King is gone, the King is gone,
Weep, my Country weep, for the King.

Mourn, my Sister, mourn,
Our Brother's gone, our Brother's gone.
Weep, my Sister, weep, for our Brother.

Mourn, oh, Mother, mourn,
Your Son is gone, your Son is gone.
Weep, oh, Mother, weep, for your Son.

Mourn, Beloved land,
Our Lord is gone, our Lord is gone.
Weep, Tamera, weep, for our Lord

For your Son,
For our Brother,
For my Love.

The grieving Goddess searched and in the land of Byblos, found her Lord. Hiding the body in the swamps, Aset sought assistance. In Her absence, however, Set, hunting in the swamp, discovered the body. In a furor, He dismembered the corpse of his brother, and with His godly strength, scattered the pieces throughout the Earth.

Returning to the swamp, the Lady of Magic beheld the empty sarcophagus, learned of Set's actions, and set out once more to recover the body of Her husband, this time piece by cherished piece.

She traveled the world She knew, and worlds She did not know, and one by one, She retrieved that parts of Her murdered Lord. At the site of each piece She recovered, She built a temple to the glory and remembrance of her King, that all in that country would know, remember and revere Asar.

All She found, all but one, and that She replaced with a member carved of the sacred sycamore.

She took the body of Her husband back to the beloved land, hid it once again, and sent out a call for help.

Nebet Het came, and Her son, Anpu, and Nut, Mother of the Gods.

Wife, sister, son and mother gathered together to perform a rite that was to be re-enacted through all the ages of the beloved land.

Gently, they assembled the body of Asar. With the sweetest of herbs, the most fragrant of spices, They perfumed it; in the finest of linen, They wrapped Their Lord. Then Aset and Nebet Het stood, one at the foot and one at the head of Asar, and They called to Their brother.

Lament of Aset & Nebet Het

Come back, come back,
O beautiful boy.
Come home to those who love thee.
Come back, come back,
Beloved of all,
To those who wait in mourning.
Come to thy sister,
Come to thy wife.
And bring the joy back into life.
Come to thy house
And ease the pain
Oh, let our tears not be in vain.
Come back, come back,
O beautiful boy,
Come home to those
Who love thee, who mourn thee,
Who call.

But Aset was Mistress of Magic, and She had further work to do, further spells to cast. Her power was great, and made greater still for the longing She felt for Her Lord.

Chanting Her ancient magics, She transformed Herself into a kite, spread Her wings, and hovered above Her husband. Performing the greatest enchantment of all, She brought life anew to Asar, and at the same time, conceived their son, Heru the Younger, Heru the Hawk, Heru sa Aset,Heru sa Asar.

Heru, Heru,
Young Lord, Bright Lord, Heru!

Heru, Heru,
Lord of Morning, Heru!
Heru, Heru,
Born of Aset, Heru!

Heru, Heru,
Son of Asar, Heru!
Heru, Heru,
Hawk of Heaven,
Heru! Heru! Heru! Heh!

Heru grew to manhood, and challenged Set, who had occupied the throne of Tamera. A great battle took place, witnessed by all the Gods and Goddesses known to the people of the beloved land. Among them were those who have no other part in this story, but who cannot, because I love them, be ignored.

There was the Lady of Malachite, Patroness of the Arts, She of the Horned Crown.

Het Heret

Roots reaching into the earth.
Down to the depths of the earth.
Life flowing from the world's heart
My Lady Het Heret, Thou Art.

Trees reaching up to the sky.
Trees with their limbs in the sky
Stars nestled sweet on thy bough.
My Lady Het Heret, Art Thou.

Also attending was the Cat Goddess, Dark Lady, Mother, with the eyes of Golden Flame.

Lady of the midnight fire,
Maubast.
Grant to us our heart's desire
Maubast.
Lady if you will it so
Help us learn what we must know
If our spirits are to grow
Maubast

Cat with eyes of golden flame
Maubast.
Hear us as we call thy name.
Maubast
To our waiting hearts appear
Hear us calling, Lady, hear!
Mighty Goddess, be ye near
Maubast

The mighty and gentle Lord, Khnum, also observed the battle.

The Potter's Wheel

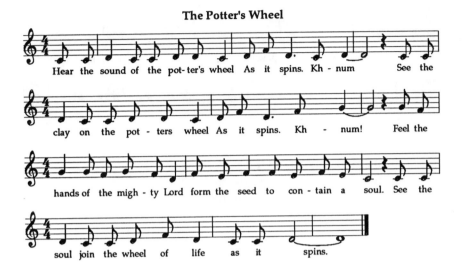

Hear the sound of the pot-ter's wheel As it spins. Kh - num   See the

clay on the pot - ters wheel As it spins. Kh - num!   Feel the

hands of the migh - ty Lord form the seed to con - tain a soul. See the

soul join the wheel of life as it spins.

Hear the sound of the potter's wheel
As it spins! Khnum!
See the clay on the potter's wheel
As it spins! Khnum!
Feel the hand of the Mighty Lord
Form the seed to contain a soul.
See the soul join the Wheel of Life
As it spins.

See the soul on the Wheel of Life
As it spins! Khnum!
Birth to death on the Wheel of Life
As it spins! Khnum!
And with death we are born anew
While the vessel that's tossed aside
Will return to the potter's wheel
As it spins!

Bes, Lord of Laughter, of Protection, the joyful warrior stood by as the battle raged.

The Dwarf

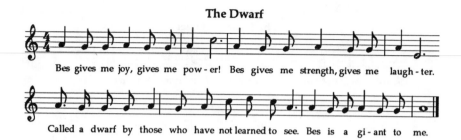

Bes gives me joy, gives me pow-er! Bes gives me strength, gives me laugh-ter.

Called a dwarf by those who have not learned to see. Bes is a gi-ant to me.

Bes gives me joy, gives me power!
Bes gives me strength, gives me laughter!
Called a dwarf by those who have not learned to see,
Bes is a giant to me.

Bes teaches joy has a power!
Bes teaches strength found in laughter!
Called a dwarf by those who have not learned to see,
Bes is a giant to me.

Heru won his battle, and regained his father's throne. From that day forth, every King or Queen claimed the name Heru during life. After death, the rulers of Tamera claimed the name Asar for He became Ruler of the Underworld, the Judge, to whom we go when we leave our bodies. For some, this is just a story, and these deities distant and unknowable. But to me, these Gods are known, and greatly loved.

The Forgotten Ones

The pyramids are old.
The ibis flies no more.
The temples have grown cold.
None come there to adore.
And Allah's name rings out
Where once Osiris was adored.
But in my heart Osiris lives
And ever is my Lord.

No more the sistrums ring
In praise of Het Heret.
No more the voices sing
In prayer to Nebet Het.
And no one thinks of lovely Nut
When stars shine high above.
But in my heart these Ladies live
And ever have my love.

Forgotten are the Gods
In lands They called Their own.
Where once a hundred lived
They call one god alone.
But in our hearts they are alive,
And ever shall They be!
O Ancient ones of Egypt, we
Have not forsaken Thee!

PART III

MAGICAL WORK—EGYPTIAN STYLE

MAGICAL TOOLS

To the Tameran, the physical world and the "Other-world" were not the separate places our culture finds them to be. The people of Tamera were aware we live in both while we're incarnate.

Many of the procedures in the Book of Coming Forth by Day, better known to us as the *Book of the Dead* seem to be designed specifically for use in the after life. I have come to believe this is not so. Many of these rituals can be used by living practitioners. For example, the various transformations into other life forms can be used to give certain shapes to your astral body in order for you to travel to specific places on the astral plane.

An entire book could be written on this approach to these ancient practices. Indeed, such a book has been written: *Coming Into the Light*, by Gerald and Betty Schueler, published by Llewellyn. There is no purpose in my repeating their work.

While most magical workings performed by Tameran magicians do not apply to us today, here are some we can use.

AMULETS

The Tamerans were great believers in amulets of many kinds, each of which had a specific purpose. Amulets were carved from stone, cast from metal, created from clay. All this is very well if you have the skills to do that, but many of us don't. Fortunately, it was also believed that the symbol, drawn on paper, was just as effective as any other form.

This is good for other reasons. You can draw several amulets on a small piece of paper and carry it in your purse or wallet. Carrying several stone amulets (should you feel the need) could ruin the cut of your suit, or make your purse very difficult to carry!

Below, several of these amulets are discussed. If you have the skills, of course, you could make them out of clay or metal or stone. If you are like me, drawing them on paper will have to serve. I suggest that you use the parchment-colored paper available today. It has a look as close to papyrus as we can achieve, unless, of course, you can obtain papyrus.

When you have created your amulet, pass it through the smoke of incense for consecration. Whenever possible, I've included a prayer to be said at that time. The amulet will then be ready to carry or wear.

THE PAPER AMULET

This spell can be used for almost any purpose.

1. On a piece of paper, draw a picture of the deity appropriate to your purpose. As you do this, remember that to the Tamerans, drawing a picture was almost the same as invoking that deity.

2. Aloud, or on the paper, state your need or problem.

3. Ask the deity to come forth.

4. Identify yourself with the deity, feeling that you have the power of Him or Her.. "My flesh is your flesh, my bones are your bones" is one way this might be stated. Meditate on the ability of that deity to deal with your problem, and know that, having that ability, you can now deal with it.

5. When you are confident, fold the paper up, and carry it with you until it is no longer needed.

6. When the problem is solved, or the need met, burn the paper with incense, sending your thanks to the deity upon the rising smoke.

CHILDREN'S AMULET

Children were often given a strip of papyrus on which was written the statement of a deity that He or She was the protector of the child. Such a statement might read: "Heru, the Mighty, Lord of the Skies, says: Hear me, all who would bring harm to _____, whose mother is _____, whose father is _____. Know ye that this child is under my protection.

Never shall my eye be away from her/him and never shall any who do him/her harm escape my wrath. Heru has spoken."

HEART AMULET

We tend to think of our hearts in two ways, the physical heart, and the emotional one. "I couldn't find it in my heart to do it." "My heart is broken." "He has a black heart." The ancients held similar views. The heart not only pumped blood, but was the source of good and evil thoughts, and the home of the conscience.

When created for the dead, the heart amulet was made to replace the heart removed during the mummification process. A heart was necessary in the Otherworld because it gave the deceased the power to move and speak. It was also believed that, in the time of judgment, the heart was weighed against the feather of Maat, and the deceased hoped his or her heart would not have evil things to say about him or her.

You can use the heart amulet in several ways. You can use it to keep evil from being said against you. You can use it for protection. You can use it for the understanding of your own heart, and therefore your own thoughts and emotions. The prayer used in consecration would make the difference.

To prevent evil from being said against you:

"Oh, my heart, my mother; my heart, my mother! My heart whereby I came into being. Let not that which is false be uttered against me. Let none cause words of evil to spring up against me."

For protection:

"Oh, my heart, my mother; my heart, my mother! Be thou the Bennu, soul of Ra and Soul of Osiris. Let me be protected by those great Lords."

To understand your heart:

"Oh, my heart, my mother; my heart, my mother! I shall gain mastery over thee. I shall understand thee and so understand myself. Open to me that I may know thy thoughts which are my own."

THE SCARAB

Not only was the scarab used in the same way the heart amulet was, but it also had its own special attributes.

It was a symbol of the God Khephera, whose name means "Becoming, being, transformation." Used among the treasures of the deceased, it was a symbol of revivification, life after death. It is a symbol of the Sun, its never-ending cycles, and the life-giving power it has.

The sun may disappear at night, but it shines on, though we are unable to see it. Khephera is the midnight sun, and the scarab symbolizes the hidden light.

The sun reappears every morning, and the day is new—everything begins again. The scarab symbolizes that rebirth.

The ancients believed wearing or carrying a symbol of Khephera would attract all that He is. A prayer for the consecration of your amulet could be:

"Hail unto Thee, Khephera, Lord of Beginnings, whose shrine is hidden, thou Master of the Gods. Be ever present, I do ask, that I may grow and transform, that I be made new each day, so I may spend that day, as I spend each lifetime, serving Thee."

An ancient rite is described for the consecration of a scarab ring. In the prayer attached to this, you speak as Tehuti, calling Khephera forth.

Take the ring and place it on a piece of olive wood. Set both on a linen cloth. Burn myrrh and kyphi. Have a small container (tradition calls for one made of chrysolite, but do what you can) in which you have an oil of lilies, myrrh or cinnamon. After you have cleaned the ring, and purified it by passing it through the smoke of the incense, place it in the oil. Leave it for three days.

On the morning of the third day, burn incense, including some olive leaves if you can. Remove the ring from the oil.

Turn toward the east, and anoint yourself with the oil on the ring, saying:

"I am Tehuti, the inventor and founder of medicines and letters; come to me, thou that art under the earth, rise up to me, thou great spirit."

Any time you feel the need, you can, in the morning, reanoint yourself by dipping the ring in the oil. According to my sources, the proper days to do this are the 7th, 9th, 10th, 12th, 16th, 21st, 24th and 25th days of the month. If you are skilled enough to make your own ring, carve a symbol of Aset on the bottom.

THE KNOT OF ASET

This symbol is also known as the "Blood of Isis" or the "Girdle of Isis." It is used for the purpose of invoking Her protection. When carved from stone, the stone is usually red. If you make a parchment amulet, do it in red ink, or paint it red.

The prayer below can be worded for you, or you can place the name of a friend or loved one—this would make a nice gift for one you wished Aset to protect.

"The blood of Aset, and the strength of Aset, and the words of power of Aset shall be might to act as powers to protect me, Her Child, and to guard me from him that would do unto me anything

I hold in abomination."

THE PILLOW

This is a wonderful amulet to make for someone who is ill, especially if you have done healing work for him or her.

If you don't know how to do healing work, you can sit quietly, picturing your friend strong and well, seeing healing energy surrounding your friend. When this is done, prepare your amulet, and bless it with this prayer:

"Thou art lifted up, O sick one that lies prostrate. They lift up thy head to the horizon, and thou dost triumph by reason of what was done for thee."

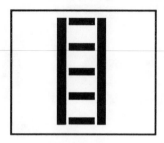

THE LADDER

When used for one who is deceased, the Ladder was intended to help that person ascend to heaven. I use it to help me reach upward toward the Gods, to learn from Them, and grow toward Them.

Say over the amulet:

"Homage to thee, O Divine Ladder. Homage to thee, O Ladder of Heru, of Asar, of Aset. Stand thou upright, O Divine Ladder, and lead me to that which is my goal."

THE NEFER AMULET

This is a good luck amulet. It is the hieroglyph for "beautiful" and "good." Ask the blessings of any or all of the deities as you pass it through the smoke.

THE MENAT

The menat is a symbol of balance, and therefore joy, and health. (See the section on Het Heret for more information.) Ask the blessings of Het Heret as you consecrate it.)

THE SHEN

This symbol of eternity is intended to give life as long as the Sun continues its orbit. Ask the blessings of the Sun God you prefer.

THE TWO FINGERS

These represent the two fingers Heru used to help Asar up the ladder to heaven. Make it to symbolize help you wish from the gods, or give it to a friend who needs that help.

THE FROG

This glyph not only represents the Goddess Hekat, but also means "myriads" or "100,000." It is connected with childbirth, and rebirth. Use it to assure a healthy child, or for good luck.

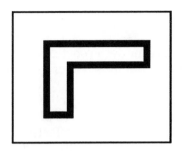

THE NEHA AMULET

This symbolizes protection. Call upon whatever deity you wish for that protection as you consecrate the amulet.

WAX FIGURES

The wax figure made infamous by some modern practices can be used in beneficial ways, and was in the Two Lands. Wax figures were a very important tool to the Tameran magician.

The figure should be prepared to resemble the subject of the spell. You can incorporate the usual personal items—pieces of fingernail, hair—into the figure to make the spell more effective. When the figure is ready, incise the name or image of a deity on the figure to give the subject the power of that deity. If you are doing a healing, carve an ankh. (If you are thinking about using this spell in a harmful way, shame on you.and remember that what's going out is what's coming in!) The figure can be given to the subject, or put in a safe place.

USHABTI FIGURES

These small figures, made to resemble their owner, have been found by the thousands in various tombs, but have also been found in houses. They are magical servants in this life as well as the next. Except for the fact that they have an existence on this plane, and are created as permanent servants rather than having life only for the duration of a specific errand, I'd call them "fetches."

Unlike the ushabtis designed to do physical work for their owners in the Otherworld, these cannot do the gardening or house-cleaning for you, but they can do "other plane" work. They can find things for you, serve as protection or sources of energy, etc. You can create these little self-images of clay, wood or cloth. If they are designed for a specific purpose, you should keep that work in mind as you design them, and the figure should be in a form prepared to do that work. For example, if you want it to search out ideas for paintings, the figure should be an artist, perhaps holding a brush.

When the figure is complete, charge it to do the work you want it to do and put it in a safe place. (See the section on rituals.)

CREATING A SISTRUM

I have many talents, but the kind of work involved here is not among them. These instructions come from Chris, my husband and High Priest.

The simplest sistrum, and probably the most ancient, is made with a forked stick. To make this sistrum, you will need such a stick, a coat hanger or two, metal washers, and wooden or metal beads.

Drill four holes on each side, spacing them evenly and making sure that the holes on one side are opposite the holes on the others. These holes should be big enough for coat-hanger wire to pass through loosely (Illo 1).

From a coat hanger, cut four straight pieces, each 2 inches longer than needed to pass completely through the matching holes. With pliers bend each of the wires at a 90 degree angle on one end (Illo 2).

Place the straight end of the first wire through one side of the sistrum. String several washers and beads, alternating them. Place the wire in the other hole and bend the end of the wire as you did the other end, but in the opposite direction (Illo 3).

Do the other wires the same way.

For a more "formal" sistrum, you'll need the following materials:

A strip of thin copper or brass about one inch wide, and 18 inches long. It should be flexible enough to bend by hand.

A wooden dowel approximately 8 inches. Whatever finish you intend to apply should be done before you begin putting your sistrum together. The finish is up to you. I like a natural stain. I've seen a beautiful sistrum that was done in gold leaf.

A block of wood, approximately 1 1/2" x 1/2" x 6," finished like the dowel.

Coat hanger or similar wire cut in four 8 inch pieces.

1. Lay the metal out flat and mark it as shown below (Illo 4).

2. With an awl, punch or drill holes where indicated.

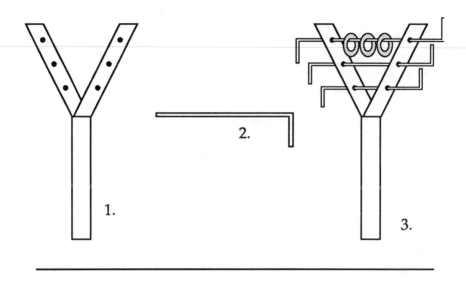

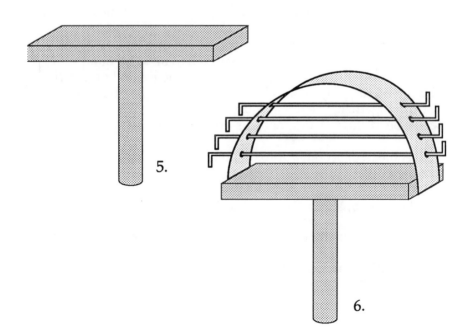

The eight holes along the length of the metal should be large enough for the wire to pass through easily. Remember, you want this wire to move when you shake the sistrum.

3. Drill a hole in the center of the block of wood the size of the dowel.

4. Place wood glue in the hole, then push the end of the dowel into the hole. Let dry (Illo 5).

5. Using nails or small screws, affix both ends of the metal first to the bottom, and then the sides of the block of wood.

6. With pliers, bend one end of each wire up in a curve.

7. Thread each wire through matching holes in the sistrum, and bend the straight end of the wire down (Illo 6). (The shape of the wire is, according to my sources, significant magically. Chris says it represents the two polarities.)

Although most sistrums seemed to have only the wires, I have seen some in which the wires held disks of metal, separated by beads, as in the first sistrum described above. You may, of course, place these on the wire before you place it through the second hole. I have one of each type—the first made per these instructions, the second with copper washers and beads the color of lapis lazuli.

CREATING A SCARAB

Only the ankh is more easily found today than the scarab. I personally have a silver scarab ring, one carved out of hematite, one made for me from clay by a friend, and twenty or thirty brown or blue-green scarabs obtained from other sources.

If, however, you want to make a scarab for your own use, a stylized one is very easy.

You will need an oven-fired clay. There are several brands of this clay available at various handicraft stores. Look for one that can be baked in the oven, usually at around 275 degrees. Some of them come in many colors. Roll the clay into a football shaped piece. Press it down on a hard surface slightly to flatten it a little. Remove the points.

Incise a "T" shape on the top.

On each side, draw three diagonal lines (legs).

On the front, draw two vertical lines.

Bake per the instructions that come with the clay.

MAKING A KILT

Although in Sothistar we do not wear Tameran garb in ritual, you might wish to wear something reminiscent of the beloved land in your rites.

In Tameran drawings, The kilt is shown two lengths—short, for every day wear or warriors, and long as the priests wore them. (Priests also shaved their heads—that's up to you. As a matter of fact, they shaved all their body hair.)

If the ladies among you wish to wear a kilt, you could wear a floor length version with a breast band, broad "suspenders," or nothing at all.

The technique is quite simple. You'll need a piece of material that is one and a half times your waist measurement, plus two inches. This allows for a one inch hem. The length of the material should be the length you wish the kilt to be plus four inches.

Lay the material flat. On one edge of the bottom, mark and cut a curve (Fig 1). Fold down the top (waist) three inches and hem. Hem all the way around the rest of the kilt (Fig 2).

Attach snaps or Velcro as shown on Fig 3.

To wear the kilt, place the straight side at your side, wrap the kilt around the front of your body, around the back, and across the front. Fasten.

This looks best if the material is somewhat stiff.

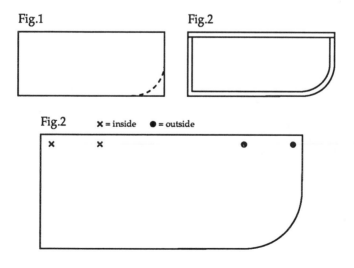

Fig.1   Fig.2

Fig.2   ✗ = inside   ● = outside

MAKING A NEMYSS

The material is cut in the shape of a truncated pyramid. The top is the narrow edge and the bottom the wide. The distance from the top to the bottom should be about 14 inches—more if you like.

Measure across your forehead and slightly down toward the nape of your neck. The "top" should be two inches larger than the measurement of your head.

From each end of the top, cut at about a 45% angle to the bottom.

Hem all the way around, making about a 3/4 inch hem.

Sew several inches of ribbon or bias tape to each side of the top.

To wear, place the top of the nemyss against your forehead, bring the ties around to the back under the rest of the nemyss and tie.

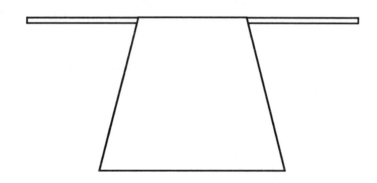

MAKING A MAGIC WAND

Although Tameran magicians did use wands, they did not resemble those you might be familiar with. These wands were different both in shape and purpose. They did not seem to be elemental symbols as they often are for those of us in the Craft. But for drawing magic circles.

Tameran wands were curved and flat, usually carved from ivory. (We, of course, would never use ivory, would we?) I can find no information on size, but the wands described in my references were found in a box that measured 18" x 12" x 12".

They were inscribed to invoke the protection of specific deities for those circles. I believe the word "draw" must not be taken literally here. A wand large enough to use standing would have to be too large to go into that box. A smaller wand would require bending over or crawling around the circle. A better (and mre graceful) way would be to hold the wand by one end and project energy through it by visualizing the energy in the form of light flowing from your hand through the wand to the floor, inscribing there a circle.

Because magical tools are only that, tools, and magical only because of their symbolism and the energy you place in them, you could make a wand out of any material you have the skills to work with, from wood to a heavy cardboard. The important thing is your concentration and the work you put into this wand.

As you cut it out, concentrate on your reason for creating a wand and on the deity or deities whose protection you wish to invoke.

After you create the wand, write on it (or draw the symbols for) its magical purpose.

If you wish to use hieroglyphs, the sentence below says "May I be in Thy protection." If you precede this sentence with the glyph for the name of the deity, you'd have a fine invocation.

Take time and decorate your wand carefully, thinking always of its purpose and the deity you wish to invoke. (This is true of all magical tools.)

When your wand is complete, consecrate it by casting a circle, raising the wand on high, and asking the deity to bless your wand so that it may serve as a proper tool to draw your protective circle.

HIEROGLYPHS

Medu neter, "the words of the God," known to us as the hiero-glyphic alphabet, consists of 30 "letters," representing 25 sounds. Most of these glyphs have existed since predynastic times.

As beautiful as they are, the hieroglyphs are not really an effi-cient way to transcribe words, but I've included them for two rea-sons. First, you might like to use them for special purposes. When Chris became High Priest of Sothistar, we gave him a cloth-covered Book of Shadows, embroidered with a cartouche of his Craft name.

Second, I believe the hieroglyphs had meanings beyond the sounds they represent. Time has not allowed me to study these hid-den meanings, but it is an area I hope to explore in the future. What thoughts I do have on the subject are included with the letters.

Hieroglyphs may be written in any direction—right to left, left to right, top to bottom, bottom to top. This allows for artistic arrange-ments. The animals and human figures face toward the direction from which the words should be read. In other words, you read toward the faces. Tameran, like English, has its homonyms. Unlike English, Tameran has a way to show which meaning applied to the word. At the end of the phonetic spelling, an additional glyph, the "determinative," would be added.

For example, my last name, Reed, is also the name of a plant. Phonetically, the word would be written:

To tell the reader the word designated the plant, a determina-tive would be added:

If, however, we meant me, we'd add a female figure:

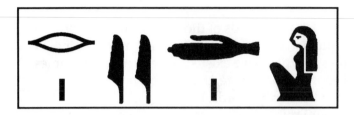

The information on how we learned to translate hieroglyphs into modern alphabets is available in many books. If you wish to learn about this, please check the bibliography. Knowing which glyphs meant which letter does not always tell us how a word was pronounced, however. So how do we know? Nobody's speaking this any more. Nobody's speaking Tameran exactly as it was spoken, but there is a "living" language, Coptic, which is basically Tameran written in the Greek alphabet, with a few new letters developed for sounds that did not exist in Greek. Almost inevitably there have been changes in the language, but this gives us an opportunity for an educated guess.

Budge has a tendency to compare the glyphs to Hebrew letters. However, there is some difficulty determining how the individual Hebrew letters were pronounced. I do my best, do what feels right, and it would seem the God and Goddesses understand. If I'm not pronouncing Their names correctly, They still respond. The list below is taken from Budge's books and S. A. B. Mercer's book *Egyptian Hieroglyphic Grammar*, and information from William Bentley, creator of a Hieroglyphics word processor. I've tried to give you the widest possible scope. Some of these letters are also words, and have meanings by themselves.

HIEROGLYPH   LETTER

A as in "Barry." There are two hieroglyphs for the letter "A." Budge calls this first one an eagle, but other sources call it a vulture, and one of a very specific kind. This vulture is almost mute, and when it does make a sound, the sound is very weak. Budge compares this glyph to the Hebrew aleph, which is a glottal stop unless it appears at the beginning of a word, in which case it is an "uh" sound, as in "about."

A as in "day." Symbolized by a forearm.

B In her book "Her Bak," Ilse Schwaller de Lubicz brings up an interesting thought. A foot or leg) implies duality because feet come in pairs. One foot is a symbol. Two feet represent reality. The name of the Earth God, Geb, is sometimes written with two "b's." Could this mean Geb manifest?

C There is no hieroglyph for "C." Use the glyph for "S," "K," or "CH."

CH Also pronounced "Dj—" (The difference is the same as the difference between "th" in "the" and the same letters in "thin.")

D It appears to be right hand, which would symbolize sending, or giving.

E as in "Edith."

E as in "Edna."

F Some say this is a snail (without a shell), others a horned viper. I lean toward the viper because snakes hiss, and that hiss can be an "F" as well as an "S." This letter also means "he."

G This is the hard "g" sound as in "garden." The closest sound to the soft "g" is the glyph for DJ. Possibly a jar.

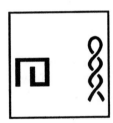

H There are two glyphs for this letter, as you see. The second is much much more energetic. They represent a reed shelter in fields, and a wick of twisted flax, respectively.

I as in "Bill" or "Michael." A reed flower.

J See DJ.

K This letter is also the glyph for "you," masculine. Basket with a handle.

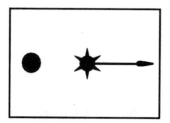

KH As in "loch," or "chutzpah" The signs seem to be interchangeable.

L There was no "l" sound as we know it in Classical Egyptian. However, we do find Greek names written in glyphs with this symbol for an "l." Dr. Mercer says it was first written with the same glyph as "r," which might tell us something about the way the Tamerans pronounced "r."

M The owl is the older symbol. The second symbol is also pronounced "ma."

N for water, ᴧᴧᴧᴧᴧ is the older symbol. It is also the word for "to" (someone) and "of."

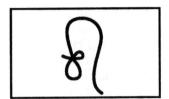

O

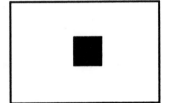

P Some sources refer to this as a door, others as a box, and still others as the top of a stool.

Q Hill slope.

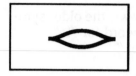

R An open mouth. I wonder if this is a comment on the pronunciation of the letter. An American "r" is pronounced with the lips pursed. Other languages roll the "r" on the tongue, with lips apart.

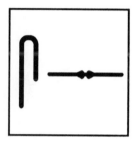

S Both signs are interchangeable. However, Ilse Schwaller de Lubicz offers an interesting thoughts ⌐ (folded cloth) is also the determinative for "health," and ――― (bolt) is the determinative for "bolt." Expansion and restriction? Would each glyph be used depending on the meaning of the word? Also means "you," feminine.

SH

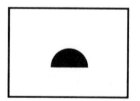

T A loaf. Often this symbol added to a word made the word feminine. (Or removing it made the word masculine, if you prefer.) For example, ▼ is "Lord," and ▼ ▲ is "Lady.

TH Tethering rope.

U Quail chick.

V There is no "V" sound. Use "F" if you wish to approach the sound closely. You could also use "U" or "B."

W Same as "U." This letter, in English, is called a "double U," and it is exactly that. If you prefer, you can use two "U's."

X There is no "X." Use "K" and "S."

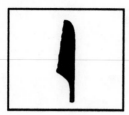

Y If pronounced as in "yahoo," use the single reed.

Z Use one of the "S" glyphs.

There are other glyphs that represent two or more sounds. Each of these is also a word, so you can use them alone or to make longer words.

HIEROGLYPH	SOUND	MEANING

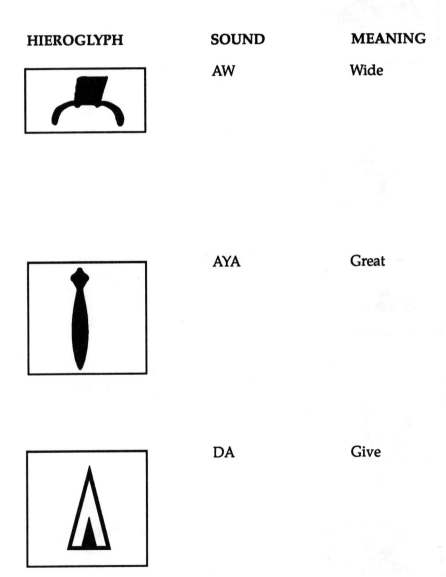

AW — Wide

AYA — Great

DA — Give

HIEROGLYPH	SOUND	MEANING
	GEM	
	HER	Face
	HOTEP	Offering peace
	KA	Spirit, life force
	KHEPER	Becoming, transformation, being

HIEROGLYPH	SOUND	MEANING
	MA	
	MEN	Firm, established
	MER	Love
	MIS, MES	Born, child (of), birth
	NEB	Before nouns, "Lord"; after nouns "all"

HIEROGLYPH	**SOUND**	**MEANING**
	NEBET	Lady
	NEFER	Beautiful, good
	NETER	God
	NETERET	Goddess
	NU	

HIEROGLYPH	**SOUND**	**MEANING**
	SA	Son
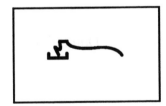	SAT	Daughter
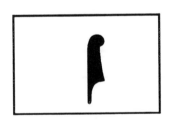	SETEP	Chosen
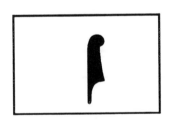	SHU	

HIEROGLYPH	SOUND	MEANING

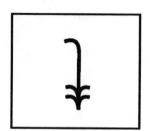

SU

TA   Land

UAS   Dominion

UN

HIEROGLYPH	SOUND	MEANING
	UP	
	UR	Great
	USER	Powerful, strong

OTHER WORDS

These are single glyphs or a combination of glyphs that form words you might find useful.

GLYPHS	MEANING
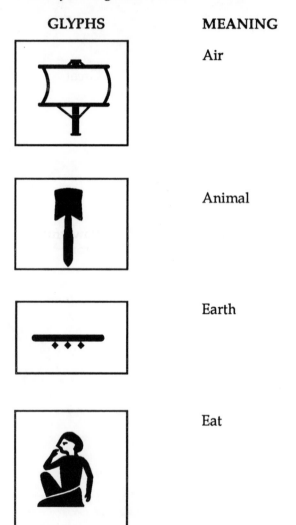	Air
	Animal
	Earth
	Eat

GLYPHS   **MEANING**

Father

Festival

Fire

God

GLYPHS   **MEANING**

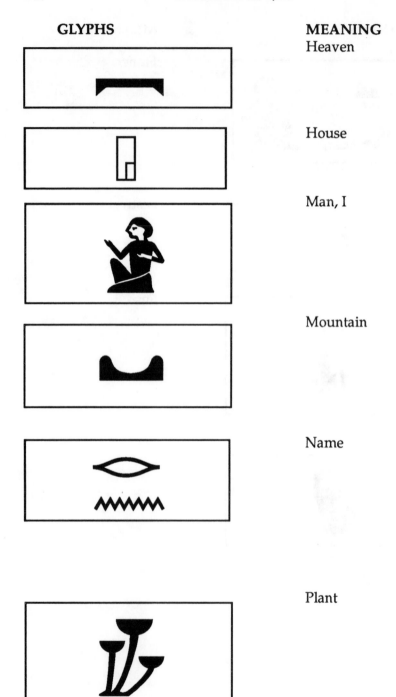

Heaven

House

Man, I

Mountain

Name

Plant

GLYPHS

MEANING

Prayer, praise

Tree

Water

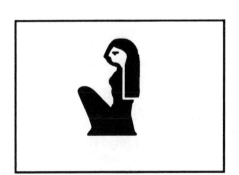

Woman

DIVINATION

In my research, I found very little on divination that could apply today. I do know the ancients used several forms of scrying. I did find the following which seems to be a method for "dreaming true."

Obtain a white oil lamp, one that will be used for no other purpose. Purify the lamp with salt, asking the blessings of the Gods (in general, or of a specific deity if you wish) and state the question about which you seek information.

When you are prepared, place the lamp on a clay brick, where you will be able to see it, and light the lamp.

Concentrate on the flame of the lamp, letting it fill your eyes and your mind. Do this until you see in the flames, something that brings a particular deity to mind, or until you feel a presence in the room with you.

At this time, lie down, and go to sleep. Be sure the oil lamp is in a place it will be in no danger of being knocked over, and let it burn throughout the night.

When you awaken, immediately make notes of your dreams and of your feelings at the moment of waking.

Thank the Gods for the wisdom they have given you, and, if it is still burning, snuff the lamp.

As I searched for other forms of divination, I found myself considering exactly what divination is, and how the various methods work. There are so many types—crystal ball, tarot cards, furthark rune staves, tea leaves—and they all work exactly the same way. They aim your mind in a certain direction, some of them distract your conscious mind with images, and they help you to open up to the sources of the information you need.

By concentrating letting your mind wander, thinking about the rock or stick or bird you were studying, you could follow your thoughts to the source of information.

It is my feeling that almost any form of divination would be suitable, if you first asked the guidance of the Gods. Which God is appropriate? You could appeal to Nebet Het, She who is the Lady of All That Is Not What It Seems To Be. Anpu is often considered the God of True Seeing. Maat, She who is Truth, could be appropriate. Tehuti, God of Wisdom, is another. Choose as your mind and heart lead you.

If, however, you wish to use a divination form that "feels" more Tameran to you, read on. I've devised two forms of divination that have served me well.

The first, "The Udjat Oracle," is the more formal of the two, and can provide more detailed information. It also takes a good deal longer.

The second, "The Pyramid of Nebet Het," is quicker, more "tactile," and provides shorter and less detailed answers.

Both require some preparation, because they do not, at this time, exist in physical form. Having to make your own, however, can only add to the efficacy of the divination tool.

THE UDJAT ORACLE

This divination tool has a background cloth, and twenty-one pieces (seven was the Tameran number of perfection, and three the number of manifestation), each bearing, on one or both sides, a word in hieroglyphs.

The background cloth has designs on both sides, and both sides will be used in the course of your reading.

Each of the glyph pieces represents an area of your life. Many have an Tameran deity attributed to them. The reasons for this will be explained in the instructions for reading the oracle.

MAKING THE BACKGROUND CLOTH

My own background cloth is embroidered. You may also use fabric paints. The finished size of the cloth is about 16 inches square. If you make it much smaller, you will have to have tiny glyph pieces, and will run into problems having enough room to put the hieroglyphs on the pieces.

Diagram 1 shows the front of the cloth. It consists of an inner square, containing the Udjat Eye (the Eye of Horus), and four corners, each containing the hieroglyphs for one of the four seasons.

Diagram 1

Diagram 2 is the reverse side. Its center is blank and each of the corners contains a symbol for one of the four magical elements.

Diagram 2

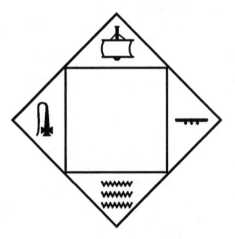

Please note: When the cloth is laid out for a reading, the top point (Spring) will be away from you, the bottom point (Autumn) will be nearest you. In other words, the cloth is viewed as a diamond, not as a square.

If you intend to embroider the cloth, you will need two pieces that will later be sewn together. If you are going to paint the cloth, either use a very heavy piece of material, or, again, use two pieces.

Unless you have the skill to draw the designs directly onto the cloth, I suggest you obtain a large pad of tracing paper and a "hot-transfer" pencil. This pencil is available at most sewing and craft stores. Used correctly, it turns your drawing into an embroidery transfer that can be ironed on to your material.

Draw your design on the tracing paper.(I found it easier to trace each part of the design separately and iron it on the proper place than to trace the whole design and try to iron it on.) When you have it exactly as you want it, flip the paper over and trace the design with the hot-transfer pencil. You'll have more success if you keep a very fine point on the pencil (I keep my sharpener handy) and use a firm, even pressure.

You are then ready to iron the pattern onto your cloth and embroider or paint it.

When both pieces are completed, sew them together, with the designs inside. Sew three sides (like a pillow case), turn it inside out, and sew the remaining side. (While you're sewing, why not whip together a bag to keep all this in?)

Take your time, place the designs carefully, and sew with care. Remember, all the energy and time and effort and work you are putting into this cloth will add to its magic. This is true of any tool you work with. Patience in preparing this cloth will reward you, not only with a nicer background cloth and a sense of achievement, but with a tool that is truly yours.

The colors you use in painting or embroidering the cloth are up to you. No one can dictate your likes and dislikes. It is important that this cloth appeal to your senses, to your heart. Because I like sparkly things, there are a lot of metallic threads in my cloth. You may prefer a little less flash, or more. Please yourself.

CREATING THE GLYPH PIECES

You have a lot of freedom when it comes to creating these pieces. I going to suggest three different methods. If you can think of another, please feel free to use it.

The first (and easiest way) is to use one of the oven-hardening clays that are available. You can find these in a natural color, or in almost any color you like. (Remember, you have to paint or ink designs on them.) My first set of pieces was made from such a clay.

I used the top of an aspirin bottle as a "cookie cutter," and found that a little large; but you might like it. You don't want your pieces too large because they'll cover too much of the cloth when you use them. Of course, you could always make the cloth larger.

This clay hardens at about 275° in the oven. When it is baked, you can sand off the rough edges, and paint it as you like.

The second way is to obtain a wooden dowel of the diameter you want, and slice it. These can be sanded, stained, and painted, inked, or woodburned. These would take a lot of work, but again, think of the magic you're putting into them! They can also be quite beautiful.

The third way is the way I did my second set. I went to a beautiful beach near San Luis Obispo, sat down, and gathered small flat stones that had been smoothed by the water. Water is very relevant to divination in my tradition, and it seemed appropriate. They are all about the same size, although they're different shapes, and I've painted the glyphs on them.

You are restricted only by your skill in the creation of your glyph pieces. The more personal the method is, the better.

You could, I suppose, cut pieces of cardboard to whatever size and shape you wish. For that matter, you could draw the background cloth on paper and use that. However, I would do so only as a temporary measure. If you're worried about putting so much effort into a divinational tool you're not even sure you'll like, remember—it would make a wonderful gift for someone!

READING THE ORACLE

Before you starting doing readings with this Oracle, become familiar with the background cloth. Lay it out before you and study it in conjunction with the pertinent diagrams.

The Udjat Eye in the center of the cloth is the Eye of Horus. It represents the Moon, as well as Protection and Wisdom. The area above the Eye represents Matters of the Spirit. The Eyebrow and the area between the Eyebrow and the Eye represents Matters in Transition. The area below the Eye deals with Matters of the Body. The iris and pupil are the Immediate Present, right now, today. The white of the Eye to the left (it would be closest to your nose if this were your left eye) is the immediate future—later today, tomorrow, etc. The white to the right of the iris (it would be closest to your ear) is the immediate past—yesterday or the day before.

At the top of the diagram, outside the inner square, is a flying beetle, the symbol of Spring. The corner to your right is the hieroglyph for Summer. Nearest you, at the bottom, is the hieroglyph for Autumn. To your left is a symbol for the Winter Solstice, the birth of the Sun.

Before you use this or any other form of divination, still your mind and ask for guidance. I imagine myself surrounded by a beautiful light, and I say, mentally, "Only higher forces around me, my Lady Aset guide me."

If your question relates to one particular area of life, find the piece that comes closest to that area. Hold it, concentrate on it; if you like, send a prayer to the God or Goddess attributed to that peice (if any). Place it with the others in the bag.

Shake the bag, or reach in and stir the runes. You can now proceed one of two ways:

1. Take about half the pieces in your hand (without looking) and toss or sprinkle them on the cloth.

2. Pull one piece at a time and place one on each of the seasons, and one in the past, present and future of each of the other divisions.

Interpret the pieces separately by meaning and placement (see Diagram 3), then interpret them in their relationship to each other.

When you have done all you can with this step, remove the

pieces, and pick out up to three that are most important.

Fold the corners of the cloth down toward the middle, forming a square (Diagrams 4-7). You will now see your elemental diagram.

Toss the retained pieces on the cloth. Their placement will tell you the type of action that will be most effective.

INTERPRETING THE GLYPH PIECES

Diagram 3 shows the meaning of the inner square. Interpret the pieces first by the meaning of the piece, and then by their placement.

If any of the pieces fall in the corner sections, representing the seasons, consult below.

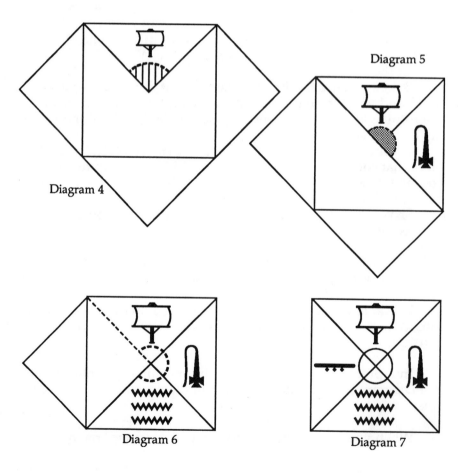

Diagram 4

Diagram 5

Diagram 6

Diagram 7

THE SEASONS

WINTER

The matter represented by the piece has not yet begun. Winter is the time of year when you choose what you will plant in the Spring. In this sense, the seed has been chosen, but not yet planted. The direction for the journey has been decided, but the first step has not been taken.

SPRING

That which is represented by the piece has begun. The seed has been planted. The journey has begun.

SUMMER

That which is represented by the piece is in progress. The seed which was planted at spring has sprouted and is taking shape. The journey continues.

AUTUMN

That which is represented by the glyph piece has become manifest. It is real. The harvest is made. The journey is completed.

THE GLYPH PIECES

ASAR

The God, male energy, positive energy, a male love interest, positive energy. When used to represent Asar as God, think more on Asar, the King, who turned his people from a nomadic tribe to the beginnings of a civilization that was mighty for centuries.

ASET

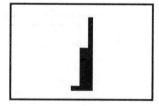

The Goddess, feminine energy, a woman, a female love interest, negative (receptive) energy. If this is in conjunction with the Magic piece, it can signify the Winged Aset, She who performed the greatest magic of all—giving new life to Her Consort, Asar, after He was murdered. In connection with the Love piece, it could signify a love interest.

NEBET HET

This piece represents all that is hidden, all that is psychic, all that is not what it seems to be. It can represent surprises, illusions and mistakes. None of these are necessarily negative. The Lady Nebet Het, whose name in Greek is Nephthys, is the dark side of the moon, hidden but existing just as surely as the side with which we are familiar. She teaches by misdirection, and Her lessons are usually learned without our even knowing we are being taught.

RA

This symbol of the Sun is one of the symbols for Ra, Lord of the Sun. This piece represents illumination. It can represent physical illumination, discovery of something on the physical plane, or it can represent spiritual illumination, that which cannot be taught or given, but comes from spiritual growth.

LOVE

Love, of course, has many forms. This piece can represent any one of them. You will have to interpret this in light of other factors in the reading. According to many sources, the Goddess of Love is Het Heret, whom the Greeks called Hat Hor.

MAGIC

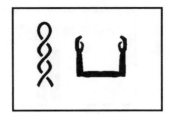

Here are the powers of the mind, the area in which you can take control, if you *will*.

WORK

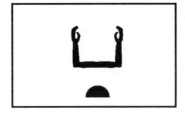

Your job or your career, the people you work with, etc. Upright could mean advancement, reversed could mean a frustration in that area. Work in conjunction with Home could mean you need to do your homework, i.e., do a little more than is expected of you.

HEALTH

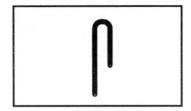

Health can also be defined as wholeness, or balance. Its meaning, like the others, can vary according to the area in which it falls. If found in Matters of the Spirit, it can imply a need for balance, or that balance exists in that area. In Matters of the Body, it can imply health, or a need for healing.

FOCUS

That on which you are focusing your attention (if upright). Reversed could imply that you should be focusing your attention there. The deity attributed here is Her Ur, Heru the Great, or Heru the Elder. He is a Sun God, but is not Heru, son of Aset and Asar. The two Udjat Eyes are, in some legends, considered to be His Eyes. The one used on your background is his left eye, the Moon Eye. Reversed, it would be the Sun Eye, also known as the Eye of Ra.

GROWTH

Upright, where growth is occurring; reverse, where growth is needed. For help, apply to Aset or Asar, or to the Lord or Lady who is most important to you.

ENERGY

Areas where energy is being applied, or should be applied.

RESTRAINT

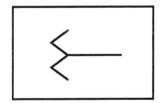

This is the area where you are restricted, or if reversed, should limit yourself.

WORDS

Learning, communication, teaching, books, science. In Matters of the Spirit, the implication would be something you are studying now. Perhaps inthe future, something you will learn. If, for example, you are looking for a teacher, it could mean finding that teacher.

Naturally, Tehuti would be the deity to call upon.

LUCK

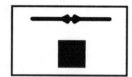

Good luck if upright, difficulties if reversed. The delightfully ugly Dwarf God, Bes, is the God of humor, home and luck. If you are interested in your destiny, your karma, there is a God called Shai. It is said that each of us have our own Shai, our own destiny.

BEGINNINGS

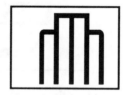

A start, if in the present or future, something that has begun, if in the past. If reversed, the same is true of endings.

The God of Beginnings is either Khephera, whose name means "becoming," or Khonsu, who is more specifically the beginnings of cycles.

FLOW

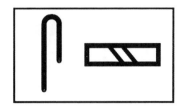

Matters in the same division of the background as this piece are flowing as they should (if upright) or not (if reversed). If this is touching or very near another, the two should be read together. The God of the Nile, Hapi, was very much involved with Flow...with the life-bringing nurturing flow of the great river.

TIME

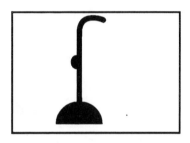

If this is touching any part of the Eye, check Diagram 8 for the number involved. It could be days, hours, etc. If it is not touching the Eye, it might mean, "Now is the time."

HOME

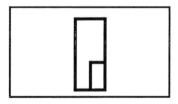

Anything to do with home or immediate family, including your dwelling place. Upright would mean pleasant or positive events. Reversed would mean problems. In combination with the Friends piece, this could mean company or entertainment in your home. This glyph appears in the names of two goddesses well-known to many of us. Nebet Het (Lady of the House) and Het Heret (House of the Sky). A more appropriate deity to appeal to, however, would be Bes.

FRIENDS

Anything to do with your friends, or the environment outside your home and your work. Upright can imply the growth of friendship. If it falls in the present, current friends can be important; in the past, old friends, and in the future, new friends. Reversed can mean that your problems stem from that friendship, or that your friends have problems and you can help.

NUMBER

If this is touching the Eye, check Diagram 8 for the number involved.

THE ELEMENTAL DIAGRAM

AIR

The problem will be handled best by work of the mind..ideas, thoughts, learning, teaching, etc. Your strength is in the wand.

FIRE

The solution is to be found in action of the will, in passion, in courage. Your strength is in the sword.

WATER

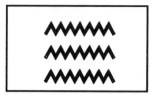

The answer lies in water, in your emotion, in nurturing. Your strength is in the cup.

EARTH

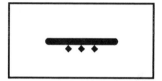

You will find the answer in Earth, physical action, steadfastness, growth. Your strength is in the shield.

SPIRIT (The center circle formed by the corners coming together.) It is in the hands of the Gods.

MEDITATION

Place the appropriate piece (or any other item) in the pupil of the eye. Focus on it, and see where your thoughts lead.

MAGICAL WORK

Choose the piece that relates to your desire, and place it on the appropriate part of the background. For example, if you want to move, place the Het (Home) piece in the space between the eyebrow and the eye, in the area that signifies the past. You may add prayers, chants, and so forth, making this spell-working as complex or simple as you wish. Light a candle and spend some time sitting before the cloth each day. During this time, visualize yourself moving. Each day, move the piece a little toward the future section. Continue the spell until you start to pack!

THE PYRAMID OF NEBET HET

Nebet Het, Lady of Things Unseen, inspired this divination tool. It uses psychic touch rather than sight or thought, and is good for simple questions. Its use is not difficult, but may require practice.

USING THE PYRAMID

Place your finger at the beginning (outside opening) of the Pyramid, just before the first glyph. Think of your question, its ramifications, the information you need, etc. then you have it clearly in mind, begin tracing your finger slowly around the Pyramid.

When one of the glyphs feels different, stop. What do I mean by "different?" No one who has used the Pyramid has used the same word to describe the feeling; "warm," "cold," "rough," "sticky," "hot," and "sand-papery" have all been said. You will, with practice, discover your own "different."

Look up the glyph your finger stopped on for the interpretation.

CREATING YOUR OWN PYRAMID

Although the Pyramid in this book can be used, it is really too small for comfortable use. You'll have better success if you reproduce it in a larger size.

There are several ways you can do this. Many photocopiers have enlarging capabilities. If you possess the artistic skills, you can redraw the Pyramid.

Once expanded, the Pyramid can be used as is, or made even better. Trace the design on heavier paper or poster board (graphite paper is available and can be erased if you like) and go over the design with the type of paint that is "puffy." This will make both the Pyramid itself and the glyphs three dimensional, and add to the tactile sensation. It will make it possible to use the Pyramid without looking at it.

Woodburning is another possiblity.

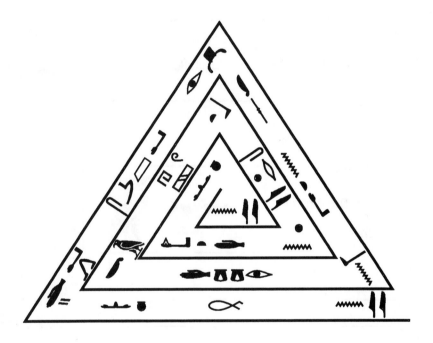

INTERPRETATIONS

YES

Energies are positive. Go ahead.

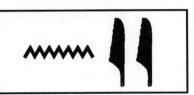

NO

Energies are negative. Stop.

MEDITATION

Meditate on the matter.

MAYBE

The answer is not known at this time.

LIE

You are not being told the truth.

TRUE

You are being told the truth.

LAW

Check the legalities before you proceed.

DANGER

Be careful. There is danger here.

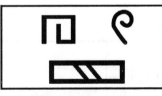

PASSING

The matter is temporary

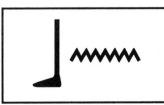

END

The matter is ended.

INFORMATION

You need more informa-
tion before you proceed.

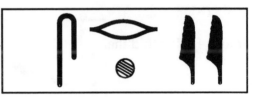

CYCLE

The matter is part of a natural cycle.

HELP

The matter should not be
dealt with by you alone.
Look for help.

WAIT

Nothing can be done at this time.

WIDE VIEW

Take the long view. Try to see how the matter can affect the big picture.

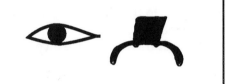

LOOK

Look at things from a different angle.

INCENSES AND OILS

Because the Tamerans Gods believed this God had a very sweet smell, the fragrance of the incense reminded them of and turned their minds toward the Gods. They also believed the smoke carried their prayers to the Gods. Thus to the Tameran, incenses saved two spirits purposes.

Many of us witches use incense often, in and out of ritual. The use of incense "just because we want to" can have one of two effects. It can lessen our feelings about the magical uses of incense, or it can bring those feelings into our every day lives. The result is up to you. Continue to use incense when the mood strikes you, but as you light it, say a small prayer. For example: "Lord and Ladies, let the fragrance of this incense remind me ever of you."

Make an effort, too, as you smell the incense, to remember that its smoke carries your words to the Gods, and take care with what you say. Say nothing you don't want Them to hear!

Use incense during any meetings you have that relate to your religion. For that matter, you could use them to set the mood for any meeting, whether or not it relates to your path.

Most of the "perfumes" mentioned in the various writings were actually scented oils. Among the scents the Tamerans were known use were myrrh, cardomom, and probably sandalwood. We know they also had sesame, coriander, a kind of calamus (sweet flag), a type of oregano, cumin, anise, and violets.

The following recipes were developed partially from research, and partially from "feel." You can, of course, use them as they are, or you can develop your own. Just as we do not necessarily view the Tameran deities as the Tamerans did, we do not restrict ourselves to plants and materials that were available to those ancients. It is more important that an incense seem right to you than it be historically accurate.

The two Aset incenses (Maria's and Ember's) reflect very different aspects of Aset, as you'll see when you use them.

EMBER'S RECIPES

Ember, as you know by now, is a member of our coven, and has developed the recipes below for the deities she knows and loves.

RA

6 parts frankincense
4 parts rosemary
1 part bay leaves

If you wish to mix this with sawdust so make it self-burning (i.e., you won't have to use charcoal), ash sawdust would be most appropriate.

BES

3 parts juniper berries
1 part bay leaves

Oak would be the best sawdust.

NUT

1 part myrrh
2 parts sandalwood

Use willow sawdust for a base.

ASET

3 parts gum benzoin
1 part lavendar
1 part cedar

Birch sawdust would make the most appropriate base.

TEFNUT

3 parts lavender
1 part spearmint

When Ember created this incense, the fragrance of the mixture seemed perfect, but when she burned it, she had the strong feeling that Tefnut objected. It came to Ember that this incense should be used as a simmering potpourri. That's most appropriate for a Goddess who symbolizes the moisture in the air, water in transition. You may find this method most appropriate for other deities, as well. One advantage to the use of this method is that the fragrance given off is closer to the smell of the herbs. Burning often changes the smell.

MARIA BLUMBERG'S INCENSES

Maria Blumberg is a friend, Craft sister, and documentary maker who created these incenses just for this book, and therefore, just for you.

ISIS

> 3 parts white sandalwood
> 2 parts myrrh
> 2 parts orris root
> 1 part rose petals
> 1 part frankincense
> 5 drops lotus oil or Bouquet (recipe below)

> Grind all ingredients to powder. Add oil or bouquet.

Bouquet
(courtesy of Scott Cunningham)

Equal parts rose, jasmine, white musk and ylang-ylang oils. Mix until scent is heavy, floral, warm.

OSIRIS

> 5 parts frankincense
> 4 parts juniper
> 3 parts dittany of crete
> 2 parts cedar leaves
> 1 part myrrh
> 3 crops lotus oil or Bouquet. (See Isis recipe.)

Grind all ingredients to a fine powder and mix. Blend in oil. If you like, color with green food coloring.

HATHOR

  5 parts orris root
  4 parts rose petals
  3 parts myrrh
  2 parts spikenard
  2 part sweet flag (calamus)
  6 drops civet oil
  9 drops henna oil (oil from the henna plant flower)

Grind all ingredients to fine powder and mix. Add oils. Blend.

BAST

  4 parts frankincense
  3 parts acacia gum
  2 parts myrrh
  1 part catnip
  1 part cedar
  1 part cinnamon
  1/2 part juniper
  2 drops civet oil

Grind ingredients to fine powder and mix. Blend in oil.

SEKHMET

  3 parts red sandalwood
  3 parts cinnamon
  2 parts myrrh
  1 part benzoin
  1 part catnip
  1/2 part Dragon's blood reed
  7 drops cedarwood oil

1 small pinch asafoetida (optional—this herb has a very strong and, to some, noxious smell.)

Grind and blend together.

FOOD AND DRINK

As is true with many covens, our celebrations usually include a pot luck feast. Whenever possible, we like to include some dish that might have been served in Tamera. If you wish to do this, or use the proper beverage or food for an offering, this chapter may be of use to you. (Offerings by the way, can be consumed later. We usually pour a liquid onto the ground, and leave the food outside for the wild animals.)

The Tamerans used a wide variety of foods, many of which are familiar to us.

BEVERAGES

The beverages most often mention in Tameran writings were water, milk, beer, and wine.

Almost any grain could be made into beer. The grain was first sprouted in, as far as I can tell, the very way we make sprouts for salads and sandwiches. The sprouts and some water were ground into a moist dough and formed into cakes. (Only one source mentions an addition of yeast.) These were lightly cooked, then broken up into water. After a day or two, the mixture would have fermented enough to be alcoholic. It was strained and drunk at this point. It kept only a day or so before it became undrinkable. If you prefer not to bother, any malt liquor will serve as well symbolically.

There is also mention in both legend and literature of "red beer." This could be red because of the grain used, or because of an additive. A legend regarding one aspect of the Goddess mentions beer either colored with pomegranate juice or ochre. There is a beer available today that is "red" and we've adopted the tradition of another organization of honoring Sekhmet by having this beer at our gatherings. I don't think it would be wise to mention the brand name, but I'll give you a hint—the name is Irish.

We have found mention of Tamerans drinking beer sweetened with honey that resembled mead. This came as no surprise to me because we had in various conversations come to the conclusion that the Tamerans could not have escaped learning about mead.

Consider the following: The Tamerans did have honey. The bees, and therefore the honey they created, were sacred to Min, God of Fertility. The Nile valley is very hot. Water mixed with honey or honey itself sitting around in jars could very easily have fermented. (I think this is how Og, the cave man discovered booze in the first place!) Surely in thousands of years someone noticed this.

If you agree, you might want to try the mead recipe below:

1 quart honey
3 quarts of distilled water

Mix and boil for five minutes. (If you wish to include herbs and spices, add them while it cooks.) Cool down to just above body temperature. Add a package of yeast and mix. Put in large container. Cover with plastic wrap or plastic bags and allow for expansion. Put in a dark place and let sit for seven days. Refrigerate until it settles (2 or 3 days). Strain and bottle. Keep in a cool dark place. This is drinkable now, but I'm told that it is even better aged for several months. We don't know at our house, because it never lasts that long. Be careful. This is no lightweight drink. It proofs out at about 60.

For those of you who do not wish an alcoholic drink, the following is a recipe for a non-alcoholic mead, again, thanks to Delphia.

1 quart honey
3 quarts of distilled water
1/2 cup lemon juice
Boil five minutes, cool, and bottle immediately.
    Keep refrigerated to prevent fermentation.

Even now there are wines available whose original grape stock came from Egypt. They are:

Malmsey— a madeira dessert wine
Rainwater madeira
Nebbilio
Amarone
Nebbilio d'Alba
Est est est
Pinot Griglo

Wines related to Eyptian wines are:
Savignon blanc—similar to wines from the Delta.
L'Tour Blanc (has a picture of a shrine to Asar on its label.

FOODS

BREADS

There are mentions of many kinds of breads mentioned in Tameran literature, and, although we don't know what all the different names mean, the breads do seem to have been both flat or unleavened breads, consisting of flour and water, and leavened breads using yeast. Rather than depend on wild air-borne yeasts, the Tamerans very probably had a type of sourdough. I have a recipe (I'll discuss its source later) for "Beer Bread" that used a 12-ounce bottle of beer as a leavening. It is possible that home-made beer was used in this way, just as bread was made to make beer.

Some skilled bakers added honey or fruit to the dough. Spices, onions and so forth could be added for a different flavor. It was then baked either on hot rocks or in an oven

FRUITS AND VEGETABLES

Onions were a very popular vegetable in Tamera, and were often eaten whole. Other vegetables commonly in use were carrots, turnips, leeks, peas, beans, lentils, spinach, and garlic. They also had watermelons. Pumpkins were popular, and since pumpkins are a type of squash, other types of squashes would be suitable. Lotus roots were also used as a vegetable, much as we use potatoes. (Check an oriental food store for these). Archaeologists have found watercress seeds in Egypt. Peppermint was also indigenous.

The fruits they used were dates, figs, pomegranates, and grapes. There is also mention of a persea tree. The avocado is a persea, and whether or not it is the same tree, we do use avocados for such feasts. (Egyptian guacamole?)

MEATS

The Tamerans definitely used beef. They did not seem to eat pork, and usually only the poor ate fish.

Along the river, wild fowl were abundant—ducks, geese, partridges and others—and Tamerans also had domesticated ducks and geese. Partridge is hard to come by in most parts of our country, so we substitute Cornish game hens. A friend who has cooked both says she finds very little difference.

The domesticated chicken was not in Tamera until the Late Kingdom. Up until that time, the eggs they used were duck or goose eggs. I confess I haven't tried either type of egg, so I can't vouch for taste, nor would I know how to obtain them. Chicken eggs will do fine.

I've recently obtained a wonderful book with recipes that could well have been used in Tamera, *The Good Book Cook Book* by Naomi Goodman, Robert Marcus and Susan Woolhandler. Any of the Egyptian recipes included in this book would make wonderful additions to a festival feast

All this is great fun to do, but the important thing in a feast is enjoyment and good taste. Be grateful to the Lord and Lady for the bounty you've received, and your feast will be traditional.

GLOSSARY

While a glossary is usually a small dictionary of terms, this one is different. In addition to definitions, it contains explanations, uses, and directions for many of its entries. I confess it's a catch-all for all the little bits of information my research has garnered and for information you might find useful.

Acacia   A tree sacred to Heru.

Ankh

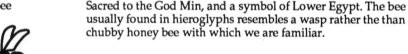

Whatever its original significance, magic knot or sandal strap, the ankh now has the meaning of"life." As a hieroglyph, it means both life and "mirror." Thus "Tutankh amen" means "living image of Amen," or "mirror image of Amen."If you chose to wear the ankh, let it symbolize life in all its aspects. Let it represent for you the choice of path, the fact that you have chosen a magical, and therefore harder path. Let it symbolize a life dedicated to growth, to service of the Gods. Let it be a sign of your respect for all life, whatever its form. Let it speak of your gratitude for the life given you by the Lord and Lady, and of your return of that gift into their hands, dedicated to Their service.

Arrow   Two crossed arrows and a shield were the symbol of Neith Uadjet also used arrows, a spear and a club. "The Archer" was another name for Tum,whose sunbeams were said to be shot like arrows.

Barque   A boat, often used to symbolize the movement of a God.

Bee

Sacred to the God Min, and a symbol of Lower Egypt. The bee usually found in hieroglyphs resembles a wasp rather the than chubby honey bee with which we are familiar.

Bennu   The Egyptian phoenix.

Black   The color was at once the symbol of theunderworld, and rebirth (confusing to some, but not to us). Not only is travel to the underworld a step toward rebirth, but black is the color of the fertile earth deposited in Tamera by the Nile.

Blood   This fluid was considered as a creative power rather than a sign of death. Legend says the cedartree spring from, the blood of Geb. See Knot of Isis.

Blue   The color of heaven, and sacred to the Gods.

Box   Magicians traditionally kept their tools in a box. One such box, belonging to a magician of the 12th dynasty, was found by an archaeologist. It contained papryi bearing magical information, four wands, a statue, three simple dolls apparently used as for spells, along with beads and amulets. Anpu was drawn on the top of the box in black vink.

Bread   It was considered one of the best offerings to make to a deity.

Brick   Most often thought of as birth bricks, on which women would stand to give birth. This birth brick was personified by Meshkenet, a Goddess whose name could be translated as "Ruler of birth."

Bull   Once upon a time, Aset told the people to choose one of the animals to be most sacred. They chose the bull, and ever after itwas one of the most revered animals in Tamera.

and   Just as the Europeans revered the stag and other large horned animals, so the Tamerans saw the strength and vitality, the masculinity of the bull, and revered it as the epitome of masculinity. In our temple, we have both types of horns, to acknowledge both our physical roots and our spiritual ones.

Cartouche   A symbol used, usually by Pharoahs, to encircle their names. It is, in reality, an elongated form of the hieroglyph "shem,"signifying eternity. It is a loop in a rope; each of our lives can be seen as contained in the loop of a rope, that rope signifying our eternal selves.

Centipede   The God Sepa, whose name means "centipede,"was called as a protection against the enemies of the Gods and noxious animals.

Child   A symbol of potential and beginnings.

Corn   The many references to corn found in books about Egypt probably refer to barley, or some other form of grain. What we in the United States call corn was not known in Tamera.

Crocodile   Considered both evil and good in Tamera.

Ears   Pictures of ears symbolized both a willingness to listen, and
                     the readiness of the Gods to symbolize prayers.

Fly   Among other things, the fly was considered a symbol of
                     courage because they are so hard to chase away. Soldiers
                     received medals in the form of the fly as rewards for bravery
                     in battle.

Frog   A symbol of Heqet, the Goddess who was portrayed as a frog.
                     She is connected with childbirth. In a relief at Denderah, she
                     is shown sitting at the feet of Osiris, an interesting statement
                     about birth and death.

Goose   Sacred to both Het Heret and Geb, the Earth God. Because the
                     egg was considered a symbol of creation, and egg-laying hens
                     were not known to the Tamerans until the 18th or 19th
                     dynasty, the goose was considered the source of creation.

Green   The color of life. If something was a good and healthy act, the
                     Tamerans said "It was a green thing to do."

Hands   You will notice in many drawings that human figures or those
                     of deities seem to have two right or two left hands. Other
                     figures have one of each, so this is not ignorance, but design.
                     The right hand signifies sending, and the left hand receiving.
                     When Nut is shown with two right hands, it shows She is
                     giving or sending energy, perhaps love, to us.

Imiut   A symbol consisting of a headless animal skin hanging on a
                     pole over a pot. It is often pictured near Asar. It could
                     symbolize the physical body left behind upon death when the
                     spirit moves on.

Incense   The use of incense in magical work was a very important part
                     of Tameran practice. They believed the smoke served as a
                     vehicle to carry prayers up to Heaven.

                     Each ingredient in an incense should be chosen carefully for
                     its magical qualities. We don't have too much information
                     about the ingredients the Tamerans used. The important thing
                     is to concentrate on the purpose for which the incense is being
                     prepared, and chose with care.

Knife   A symbol of protection and defense against evil. Ritual knives
                     were made of flint rather than metal.

Knot   In magical use, knots held magic fast. Conversely, releasing a
                        knot released the magic or its subject.

Knot of Isis   Also called "blood of Isis," it is said to resemble an ankh with
                        the arms folded down. Other sources feel it symbolizes the fal
                        lopian tubes. Usually made of a red stone such as carnelian,it
                        seemed to symbolize all that Aset represents.

Lapis lazuli   Sacred to the Tamerans because of its color. Wearing lapis and
                        gold supposedly placed one under the protection of the Sun
                        and Heaven.

Lotus   This flower is a symbol of dawn and beginnings because it
                        closes up at night and opens in the morning. It is also a symbol
                        of water. The blue lotus was especially sacred.

Malachite   Green was a joyful color to the Tamerans, and malachite was
                        said to express joy. Het Heret was called "the Lady of Mala
                        chite."

Milk   Because of its color, milk was a symbol of purity, and con
                        nected with the many depictions of a king being suckled by a
                        Goddess, thus receiving divine power.

Name   Names were as sacred to the Tamerans as they are to us. Know
                        ing someone's true name gave power over that person.

Night   The Tamerans did not consider night an evil thing, but rather a
                        door to mystery.

Phoenix   See Bennu.

Red   At some times in Tameran history, red was considered an
                        "evil" color because Set was supposed to be red-haired. If you
                        accept Set as an evil God, this makes sense. If you consider him
                        simply a Geburic figure, a God of Storm and Destruction, then
                        you cannot think of Him as evil. (Interesting that red is the
                        color of the sphere Geburah on the Tree of Life.)

                        The crown of Southern Egypt was "the Red Crown." Red was
                        born by the priestesses of Bast, and Maat's feather is red. How
                        can the color be both good and bad? Easy, we just make an
                        arbitrary decision as we often do. In some cases it is good, in
                        others, it is bad.

Ring

⊖

As it is in many cultures, the ring was the symbol of eternity.

Sa

Representing a rolled and tied herdsman's hut, this symbol ized protection.

Serpent

If life and death are part of the same thing, that which could bring death can also be a symbol of life. So it was with the ser pent in Tamera. Uadjet, the Cobra Goddess, was a symbol of power. The hieroglyph for "Goddess" is a serpent. Because it sheds its skin, the serpent also symbolized life after death.

Shield

A symbol of protection.

Ship

A symbol of transition, as in "the voyage of life."

Sistrum

An instrument used in worship, especially in connection with Her Heret.

Snake

See Serpent.

Stone

A symbol of stability and steadfastness as opposed to the short-lived ethereal nature of man.

Sycamore

A tree sacred to Nut, Asar, and Het Heret. The last was often referred to as "The Lady of the Sycamore." Its leaves used as amulets were said to bring good things to those who carried them. Sycamores were considered the manifestation of the Sky Goddess. When the tree quivered, the Gods were sitting in it.

Tongue

Because of its importance in speaking, the tongue symbolized manifestation of the will. Ptah took the creative power of his heart and spoke, manifesting his desires.

Uas

↑

A stick or wand forked at the bottom with the top resembling the head and ears of an animal, usually referred to as a "canid." (The shape of the top looks very much like Anpu to me.) Many Gods are shown holding this staff, and it has been described as a symbol of royalty and divinity. I can't help but compare this to the stang found in Celtic symbolism. This is a staff forked at the top and pointed at the bottom. It well may descend from a staff often carried by ancient tribal leaders in Europe and the British Isles. If the leader and his people approached another tribe, the position in which the stick was held conveyed their intentions. If the fork was held up, they approached peacefully; if the point was up, they approached with hostility.

A tribal leader, whatever title he or she bore was the royalty of that tribe. If that leader was also priest, he or she was the tribe's liason with the Gods. Pharoah was, to the Tamerans, both ruler and deity. I don't find these things very different. In our coven, the uas tends to be used as a masculine symbol. A priest (or priestess) will hold it when he or she wishes to serve as a vessel of the God. (The lotus wand is used for the Godess.) This does not necessarily reflect ancient symbolism. It just worked out that way.

Urshu   "Watchers," beings who watched over individuals and cities They were often messengers. To my mind, these compare to the "angels" of another mythos. They were depicted as human headed hawks wearing a solar crown and a uraeus.

Wand   Tameran magicians did use a wand, but it did not resemble one modern Witch might use. It was curved and flat, resembling a boomerang. I can find no reference to size, but we are told wands were used to draw magic circles.

Water   Symbol of life and birth.

Willow   Sacred to Osiris because it sheltered his coffin.

SOURCES

Considering the continuing fascination the world has with Tamera, it's amazing how difficult it is to find inexpensive Tameran items. (The key word here is inexpensive.)

Although I have beautiful statues of Aset, Asar, Heru, Ptah, and Anpu, they are painted plaster. There's nothing wrong with that, but research has shown it is difficult to order these through the mail. Manufacturers are reluctant to ship to individuals because shipping costs would be as much as the statues themselves. However, do check the various plaster statuary shops in your part of the world. They may well have something you'd like. If they don't, ask if you can see their catalogues. They might have more available for you. Copies of items found in Tut's tomb are available in plaster.

One of my statues of Heru was found in a thrift shop. Both of us are addicted to thrift shops and garage sales. You might be surprised what you'll find there.

Ankhs are the easiest to find, usually in jewelry form, in all price ranges. The scarab is often found in jewelry.

A wide variety of Tameran items can be found in the catalogues obtainable from museums and the Smithsonian. Many of them offer replicas of museum possessions. None of them are cheap, but worth the money, if you want the item badly enough. Send for their catalogues.

Museum of Fine Arts, Boston
Catalog Sales Department
P. O. Box 1044
Boston MA 02120-0900

This is one of my favorites. Their current catalogue offers lapis and scarab jewelry, ties with Tameran symbols on them, a mummy bean bag doll, "Pyramids and Mummies" (two games in one), mummy masks, set games, Egyptian notepads, an Egyptian puzzle, and a pin of Sekhmet.

Pick up an archaeology magazine and look through the ads. You'll find statues, large and small, and lots of other things to activate your saliva.

King Tut Creations
P. O. Box 7657
Warwick RI 02887

They offer cartouches of your name. Very expensive, but perhaps their catalogue has other items. Send them $2.00 to see.

Metropolitan Museum of Art
255 Gracie Station
New York NY 10028.

I don't have one of these, but I've seen their catalogue and it is worth sending for. Send them $1.00 and get lots of catalogues.

Hieroglyphic Word Processor. The hieroglyphs in this book come, for the most part, from this program. I have more fun with this! It is available only for the Atari ST at this point, but the programmer is working on versions for IBM and Mac. They could be available by the time you read this. The program and information on using it are available for $15. An additional disk with 92 hieroglyphs is available for $10. If you wish to create your own, you can purchase the Create program for $15.00.

Send the money to:William Bentley

P. O. Box
Santa Ana, CA 92707

You'll love it.

A Coloring Book of Ancient Egypt is available from Bellerophon books. For a catalogue, send a long stamped envelope to:

Bellerophon Books
36 Anacapa Street,
Santa Barbara, CA 93101

Ancient Egyptian Cut and Use Stencils as well as many of the books in the Bibliography can be obtained from Dover Publications. Write for a catalogue and tell them you are interested in Egypt.

Dover Publications
31 East Second Street
Mineola, NY 11501

Egyptian Designs in Modern Stitchery by Pauline Fischer and Mary Lou Smith, published by E. P. Dutton is full of wonderful needlepoint or counted cross stitch patterns.

Ares Publishers is a mail-order house as well as publisher. Several of my references came from them. Send for a catalogue.

Ares Publishers
7020 North Western Avenue
Chicago, IL 60645

Tucci International carries the lovely pictures on papyrus you may have seen. They also have a few terra cotta castings including two different cats. I prefer the larger one because it is an older version—a wild cat instead of a domestic one.

Tucci International
190 Oxford Lane #4
San Bruno, CA 94066

Sadigh Gallery carries many antiquities of interest including Egyptian ones. Ushabti figures from the 26th dynasty, mummy bead necklaces, and Egyptian neolithic flints are among the things they offer. Many of the items are affordable. If you have friends with an interest in Greek or Roman antiquities, they will enjoy the catalogue, too.

Sadigh Gallery
303 5th Avenue, Suite 1603
New York, NY 10016

Artisans Guild International. The day I got this catalogue, I called a friend to say good-bye—I was going to die of pure envy. They carry beautiful reproductions of many of the treasures of Tut's tomb, and although you don't have to be a pharoah to afford them, these people don't carry nickel and dime stuff. Most of the statues are 11" to 13" tall and most of them run about $75.00. They are "cultured" marble covered with gold leaf. In this catalogue, you'll find statues of Amen-Ra, Ptah, Aset, Nebet Het, Selket, Neith, Shu, Asar, Heru, Anpu (two of them), Het Heret, Khnum, Tehuti, and Ra-Harakhte. There is also a 6" bronze statue of Sekhmet for $25, as well as a small cat, and small ibis for the same price. The color catalogue costs $5, which is refundable with your first order. Be prepared to drool. Better yet, save up some money before you send for it.

Artisans Guild International
5610 South Soto St.
Suite C Huntington Park, CA 90255

Ancient World Arts has wonderful jewelry at reasonable prices. I said "reasonable," not "cheap." Many of their pieces are available in either silver or gold. A catalogue is available.

Ancient World Arts
50 W. Sixth Street
New York, New York 10023

If you've found other sources, don't hesitate to send word to me. We'll include them in future editions of this book.

BIBLIOGRAPHY

Larousse Encyclopedia of Mythology, London: Paul Hamlyn, 1965.

Bander, Bruce, *The River Nile*. Washington D.C.: National Geographic, 1968.

Bentley, William A. *Hieroglyphics:* Santa Ana, Bentley, 1987.

Boyland, Patrick, *Thoth, The Hermes Of Egypt*. Chicago: Ares Publishers, 1987.

Brier, Bob, *Ancient Egyptian Magic*. New York, Quill, 1981.

Bromage, Bernard, *Occult Arts In Ancient Egypt*. London: Aquarian Press, 1971.

Budge, E. A. Wallis, *An Egyptian Hierogolyphic Dictionary*, Vols. I And II. New York: Dover Publications, Inc. 1978.

——————, *Book Of The Dead*. New York: Bell Publishing Company, 1960.

——————, *Dwellers On The Nile*. New York, Dover Publications, Inc., 1977.

——————, *Egyptians Language*. New York: Dover Publications, Inc., 1983.

——————, *Egyptian Magic*. New Hyde Park: University Books,

——————, *Osiris and the Egyptian Resurrection*, Vols 1 and II New York: Dover Publications, Inc., 1973.

——————, *The Mummy*. New York: Causeway Books, 1974.

Coryn, Sidney G. P. *Faith of Ancient Egypt*. New York: Theosophical Publishing, 1913.

Cottrell, Leonard, *The Lost Pharoahs* London: Pan Books Ltd., 1964.

Donadoni, Sergio, *Egyptian Museum* Cairo. New York: Newsweek. 1978.

Drioton, Etienne, *Egyptian Art*. New York: Golden Griffin Books, 1950.

Ellis, Normandi, *Awakening Osiris*. Grand Rapids: Phanes Press, 1988.

Frankfort, Henri. *Ancient Egyptian Religion*. New York: Harper Torchbooks, 1961.

Freed, Rita E., *Egypt's Golden Age*. Boston: Museum of Fine Arts, 1982.

Harris, Geraldine, *Gods and Pharoahs*, New York: Schocken Books, 1982.

Hart, George, *Dictionary of Egyptian Gods and Goddesses*. London, Rutledge and Kegan Paul, 1986.

Hope, Murry, *Practical Egyptian Magic,*.New York: St. Martin's Press, 1984.

Lichtheim, Miriam, *Ancient Egyptian Literature*. Berkeley: University of California, 1975.

Lurker, Manfred, *Gods and Symbols of Ancient Egypt*.

MacKenzie, Donald A., *Egyptian Myth and Legend*. New York. Bell Publishing Company, 1978.

MacQuitty, William, *Tutankhamon, the Lasst Journey*, New York: Quartet Books, 1976.

Mansfield-Meade N. F., *Latest Pocketbook Guide to Luxor & Environments.* Luxor: Gaddis (Photo Stores), 1958.

Mercer , S.A.B. *Egyptian Hieroglyphic Grammar.* Chicago: Ares Publishers, Inc., 1984.

Ochsenschlager, Edward, *Egyptians in the Middle Kingdom.* New York: Coward-McCann, 1963.

Plankoff, Alexander, *Shrines of Tutankhamon.* New York: Harper Torchbooks, 1962.

Rawlinson, George, *History of Ancient Egypt.* New York: John B. Alden, Publisher, 1886.

Saleh, Mohamed, *Egyptian Museum, Cairo.* Official Catalogue Cairo: Organization of Egyptian Antiquities, 1987.

Sauneron, Serge, *Priests of Ancient Egypt.* New York: Grove Press, Inc., 1960.

Scheuler, Gerald and Betty, *Coming Into the Light.* St. Paul: Llewellyn Publications, 1989.

Schwaller de Lubicz, *Isha, Her Bak*—Volumes 1 and 2. New York: Inner Traditions, 1978.

Schwaller de Lubicz, R. A., *Esotericism and symbol.* New York: Inner Traditions, 1985.

Shorter, Alan W., *Egyptian Gods, A Handbook.* North Hollywood: Newcastle Publishing, 1935.

Smith, William Stevenson, *Ancient Egypt.* Boston: Beacon Press (Boston Museum), 1961.

Stewart, Desmond, *Pyramids and Sphinx.* New York: Newsweek, 1977.

Sykes, Egerton, *Everyman's Dictionary of Non-Classical Mythology* London: J. M. Dent & Sons Ltd.

Thompson, Herbert and Griffith, F. Ll., The Leyden Papyrus, New York: Dover Publications, 1974.

Watterson, Barbara, *Gods of Ancient Egypt*. New York: Facts on File, 1984.

West, John Anthony, *Serpent in the Sky*. New York: Julian Press, 1987.

White, J. E. Manchip, *Ancient Egypt, Its Culture and History*. New York: Dover Publications, Inc., 1970.

Woldering, Irmgaard, *Art of Egypt*. New York: Greystone Press, 1963

INDEX

Aabit 97
Aah 97
Air 60, 61, 63
Aker 97
Allah 205
Altar 7
Amen 36, 97
Amen-Ra 36
Ami 98
Ami Neter 98
Ami Pe 98
Amit 21
Amu 98
Amulet
  children's 209
  frog 216
  heart 210
  ladder 214
  menat 215
  nefer 214
  neha 217
  paper 209
  pillow 213
  shen 215
  two fingers 216
Amun 74
Amutnen 98
Anpu 11 24, 26, 35, 41, 42, 44, 122, 124, 138, 141, 154, 185-186
Anubis 11
Apache tear 24, 42
Apeleius 17
Apuat 44, 99
Aput 99
Arianrhod 11
Asar 11, 20-25 26, 35, 42, 49, 63-65, 72, 83, 123, 125, 126, 128, 130, 131, 132, 133 135, 137, 138 140, 142, 143, 146, 147, 154, 157, 158, 159-160, 164, 166, 172, 180-181, 191-200, 204, 256, 259, 276
Asar bed 22
Asar's backbone 23
Asbit 99
Aseb 99
Aset 11, 14-17, 26-28, 49, 63, 64, 72, 83, 121, 122, 126, 127, 128, 131, 133, 136,

137, 144, 155, 157-158, 160, 164, 166, 171, 191-193, 195, 195-200, 212, 256, 259, 270, 271
Ashkit 99
Ashu 100
Aswan Dam 117
Aten 118
Athame 157
Athena 11, 94
Atum 110, 128
Aua 100
Auit 100
Avenger 84
Azurite 16

Ba-Neb-Dedet 127
Bait 100
Baket 100
Barleycorn 22
Bast 8-9, 17, 30-33, 67, 123, 127, 130, 132, 134, 135, 146, 148, 202, 273
Bast, Priestess of 33
Bata 100
Beer 23, 124, 274, 275
Beginnings, Lord of 211
Bekhkhit 101
Beloved Land 4
Benevolent King 64
Bennu 210
Bes 54-59, 164, 204, 260, 261, 271
Betelgeuse 22
Bird Goddess 103
Birth, Goddess of 107
Blacksmith God 104
Blood of Isis 212
Blumberg, Maria 272
Book of the Dead 208
Budge, E.A. Wallis 12
Bulls 1, 120

Cairo Calendar 117
Cat 32-33
Cat Goddess 33, 107, 202
Celtic 3, 11, 35, 75
Celtic Gods 12
Cerridwen 11
Challenger 41

Chant 8-9
Cheops 13
Chesed 64
Childbirth, Goddess of 101, 105
Chris 42, 47, 50, 57
Chrysocolla 16
Chrysolite 212
Cobra Goddess 111, 119
Contact rituals 8, 9, 174-177
Coptic 228
Corn 22
Corn mummy 22
Cosmic Egg 78
Cow 16
Cow Goddess 108
Craftsmen, God of 68
Creatrix 15, 38
Crocodiles 118, 120, 124
Crone 12, 31, 67
Crook 21, 22, 75
Crown
　Atef 21
　Solar 15, 16
　White 21, 124

Danu 93
Dark Aset 27
Dark Lady 31, 32, 66, 201
Dark Lord 41
Dawn God 98
Dawn's Light, Goddess of 101
Death and Resurrection, Lord of 23
Death, Lord of 21, 25
Destiny, God of 109
Diana 11
Divination 248-249
Divine Potter 77
Drawing Down the Moon 7
Dung beetle 81
Dwarf 54
Dynasty, 12th 32

Earth God 12, 53, 97
Earth Goddess 10
Earth, Lord of 52, 53
East Wind, God of the 102
Eater of Hearts 21
Egyptologists 8, 176
Elements 175
Embalming, God of 112
Ember 3, 24, 46, 49, 57, 167, 271-272

Epagnomenal days 117
Existence, God of 111

Feast of the Lamps 120
Feather of Maat 20, 38, 39
Felis capensis 32
Fertility, God of 101, 275
Festival of the Dead 120
Fetches 218
Fields, Lady of 93
Fire 90
Fire God 98, 99
Fire Goddess 99
First Degree 27
Fish God 108
Fitzgerald, Edward 3
Flail 21, 22, 75
Four Fold Feast 55
Freya 11, 17

Geb 49, 52-53, 127, 138, 141, 146, 154,
　157, 158, 161, 188, 189
Geburah 64, 67
Girdle of Isis 212
Gods, Father of 52
Gods, Mother of 49, 50, 93
Golden Ass 17
Grain God 106
Grandfather 53
Grandmother 53
Grant, Joan 66
Great Pyramid 13
Griffin 105
Guardian 41, 42
Guide 41

Hags 31, 67
Hapi 101, 135, 261
Hare 187
Harvest, Goddess of the 108
Hat Hor 12, 33, 71-73, see Het Heret
Hathor 11, 273, see Het Heret
Hawk 15, 36, 83-85, 187
Hawk Goddess 100
Hearing, God of 109
Heaven 216
Heaven, House of 72
Hecate 11, 31, 32
Hedj-Hotep 119, 122, 130
Heh 101
Hekat 78, 101, 166, 216

Heliopolis 130
Henkheses 102
Heqet see Hekat
Her Bak 229
Her Ur 72, 122, 150, 154, 160, 191, 259
Heru 15, 17, 72, 83, 119, 121, 123, 128,
    130, 137, 140, 142, 144, 146, 150, 153,
    157, 172, 200, 204, 216
Heru sa Aset 36, 83-85, 136, 144
Hesa 102
Het Heret 11, 13, 16, 17, 71-73, 125, 129,
    130, 148, 149, 201, 205, 257, 261
Het Heru 13, 72
Hieroglyphs 46, 50, 183, 184, 227-247
High Lady 27
High Lord 21, 27
Hope, J. Murray 39, 43
Horus 75, 83-85, 143, see Heru, and
    Heru sa Aset
Horus the Elder 72, see Her Ur
Hour after Sunset, Goddess of the 103
Hour before Dawn, God of the 103
House, Lady of 26
Hu 102, 135
Hutchai 102

Ibis 45, 205
Imhotep 102
Incenses 270-273
Infinity, God of 101
Isis 1, 11, 14, 17-18, 169, 212, 272, see
    Aset

Jackal 41, 44, 187, 196
Jester 58
Judge 20
Justice 37

Kali 31
Keku 103
Kekui 103
Kekuit 103
Kernnunos 11
Kestrel 83
Khensu, see Khonsu
Khephera 36, 81-82, 142, 169, 211, 260
Khnum 77-78, 139, 164, 202, 203
Khonsu 74-76, 144, 260
Khufu 13
Khurab 103
Kilt 223

Kite 15, 187
Knot of Aset 212
Knowledge, Goddess of 107

Lapis lazuli 21, 22, 24, 180
Life, Lord of 25
Light, God of 107, 111, 112
Lion 187
Lioness 88, 90
Lion God 98, 104
Lotus 110
Lycopolis 44, 99
Lynx Goddess 104

Maa 105
Maat 20, 37-39, 62, 127, 133, 145, 150,
    152, 249
Maat kheru 39
Mafdet 104
Mage 191
Magic 1, 2, 15, 27
    black 57
    Lady of 198
    Mistress of 101, 200
    wand 225-226
    Worker of 15
Magician 1
Mahes 104
Maiden 12
Malachite 16, 71
Malachite, Lady of 71, 201
Malt liquor 23
Mars 64
Mathit 104
Meditation 3, 8, 10, 23, 31
Medu neter 46, 227
Menat 72
Menthu 105
Mercer, S.A.B. 228
Merseger 103
Mesen 104
Meskhenet 105, 164
Messenger God 99
Milk Cows, Goddess of 97
Milky Way 49, 188
Min 105, 137, 141, 152, 154, 275
Mockingbirds 83
Monthu 105
Montu 105, 122
Moon 16, 27, 32
Moon God 74, 97

Moon, Goddess of the 112
Morrigan 11, 17, 31
Mother 12, 15, 33, 53
Mother, Earth 53
Mother Goddesses 31, 33, 86
Mother, Sky 53, 159
Mummy 21
Mut 74, 86-87, 151
Myrrh 212, 270, 271, 272
Mystery 27

Nebet Het 11, 17, 26-28, 42, 49, 64, 127,
    133, 155, 157, 160, 171, 182-183, 191,
    195, 205, 248, 249, 257, 261, 264
Nefertum 110
Neith 94-95, 124, 130, 136, 138, 148
Nekhbet 106
Nemyss 224
Neper 106
Nephthys 11, 26, 257, see Nebet Het
Nerit 106
New Kingdom 36
Nile 117, 118
Nile, God of the 101
Nu 106
Nuada 11
Nun 106, 124, 125, 135, 139
Nurses and Children, Goddess of 99
Nut 36, 49-51, 121, 139, 148, 154, 161,
    188, 189, 191, 198, 271

Obsidian 33, 42
Odin 11
Oils 270-273
Omar Khayam 3
Opals 43
Orion 16, 22
Oryx 187
Osiris 11, 20-25, 75, 131, 169, 192, 205,
    210, 272, see Asar
Ostrich feather 37, 61, 90, 174
Owls 38, 82

Pakhit 107
Pan 56
Papait 107
Papyrus 46
Peregrine falcon 84
Pestit 107
Pestu 107
Power, Lady of 66

Priest 7, 34, 42
Priestess 7, 14, 28, 34
Primal Ocean, God of the 106
Primal Water 106
Ptah 68-70, 74, 94 128, 137
Pyramid of Nebet Het 249, 264

Qabala 64
Qeshet 3, 24, 37, 57

Ra 21, 34-36, 118, 119, 120, 121, 122,
    123, 124, 125, 126, 128, 129, 130, 132,
    134, 135, 142, 143, 144, 146, 147, 148,
    150, 153, 154, 189, 190, 210, 257, 271
Racy, Jihad 187
Ravens 83
Rekhit 107
Remi 108
Remnit 108
Renenutet 108
Renpiti 108
Rhiannon 11, 17
Roadrunners 83
Romans 17
Rubiyat 3

Saa 109
San Fernando Valley 83, 88
Sarcophagus 197
Satan 64, 66
Saturn 64
Scales of Maat 39
Scarab 81, 211-212, 222
Scheuler, Gerry and Betty 208
Schwaller de Lubicz, Ilse 229
Scorpions 3
Scribes 46, 47
Sea Goddess 17
Sebek 129, 136
Sefket 79
Seker 138
Sekhmet 65-67, 121, 129, 130, 132, 135,
    143, 155, 161, 191, 193, 197, 273, 274
Seshat 79-80
Set 22, 26, 49, 63, 64, 65, 66, 119, 120,
    121, 128, 135, 139, 142, 143, 155, 161,
    191, 193, 197
Setem 109
Setting Sun, God of the 110
Shai 109, 260
Shava Shadar 3, 23, 24

Shesmu 110
She Who Loves Silence 103
Shu 60-62, 127, 133, 148, 174
Sia 109
Sight, God of 105
Simara 3, 27, 28
Singing God 98, 102
Singing Goddess 97
Sirius 16
Sister 15
Sistrum 33, 205, 219-221
Sky Goddess 72
Sky, House of the 72
Smith Gods 77
Sobek 110, 120, 143
Sodalite 51
Solar Goddess 67
Sopdet 16
Sothis 16
Sothistar 3, 17, 21, 27, 36, 117, 223
Soul, Goddess of the 100
Staff 157
Stag 1
Star Goddess 111
Storm God 64
Storm, Lord of 194
Strength, Goddess of 106
Summerland 23
Sun 16
Sun God 12, 259
Sunrise, Goddess of 107
Sunset ceremony 120
Swallow 15, 187

27th Day of the Month, Goddess of the 111
29th Day of the Month, God of the 113
Tait 110
Tamera 4
Tanent 10, 92-93
Tannenet 128
Tao 38
Tapestry 39
Tara 93
Taste, God of 102
Tauret 110
Tayet 130
Tefnut 88-91, 271-272
Tehuti 45-47, 121, 122, 124, 128, 130, 134, 135, 139, 145, 148, 183-184, 191, 212, 249, 260

Temple of the Elder Gods 9
Tet 23, 131, 135
Thor 11
Thoth 45, 120, see Tehuti
Throne 15
Time God 108
Touch, God of 109
Tree Goddess 72, 104
Truth 37, 38
Tum 36, 110
Tutankhamen 74

Uadjet 111
Udjat Eye 249, 252, 259
Udjat Oracle 249
Un 111
Underworld, Lord of 20, 24
Underworld, Ruler of 204
Unit 111
Unta 111
Untabi 111
Unti 112
Upuat 99
Ur-Henu 112
Utchait 112
Utekh 112
Utet-tefef 113

Vegetation, Lord of 21
Vulture 15, 86, 87
Vulture Goddess 106

Wand 157
War and the Chase, God of 100
War God 105
War Goddess 94
Water 64
Water God 100, 112
Weaving, Goddess of 110, 119
West Wind, God of the 102
Wicca 7
Wife 15
Wilson, Robert Anton 58
Winds, Goddess of the 99
Wine, God of 110
Wisdom, Lord of 45, 191
Wolf 44
Words, Lord of 191

Yule 36

STAY IN TOUCH

On the following pages you will find listed, with their current prices, some of the books now available on related subjects. Your book dealer stocks most of these, and will stock new titles in the Llewellyn series as they become available. We urge your patronage.

However, to obtain our full catalog, to keep informed of new titles as they are released and to benefit from informative articles and helpful news, you are invited to write for our bimonthly news magazine/catalog. A sample copy is free, and it will continue coming to you at no cost as long as you are an active mail customer. Or you may keep it coming for a full year with a donation of just $7.00 in U.S.A. & Canada ($20.00 overseas, first class mail). Many bookstores also have *The Llewellyn New Times* available to their customers. Ask for it.

Stay in touch! In *The Llewellyn New Times'* pages you will find news and reviews of new books, tapes and services, announcements of meetings and seminars, articles helpful to our readers, news of authors, advertising of products and services, special money-making opportunities, and much more.

The Llewellyn New Times
P.O. Box 64383, Dept. 667, St. Paul, MN 55164-0383, U.S.A.
* * *

TO ORDER BOOKS AND TAPES

If your book dealer does not have the books described on the following pages readily available, you may order them directly from the publisher by sending full price in U.S. funds, plus $3.00 for postage and handling for orders *under* $10.00; $4.00 for orders *over* $10.00. There are no postage and handling charges for orders over $50.00. Postage and handling rates are subject to change. UPS Delivery: We ship UPS whenever possible. Delivery guaranteed. Provide your street address as UPS does not deliver to P.O. Boxes. UPS to Canada requires a $50.00 minimum order. Allow 4-6 weeks for delivery. Orders outside the U.S.A. and Canada: Airmail—add retail price of book; add $5.00 for each non-book item (tapes, etc.); add $1.00 per item for surface mail.

FOR GROUP STUDY AND PURCHASE

Because there is a great deal of interest in group discussion and study of the subject matter of this book, we feel that we should encourage the adoption and use of this particular book by such groups by offering a special quantity price to group leaders or agents.

Our Special Quantity Price for a minimum order of five copies of *Invocation of the Gods* is $38.85 cash-with-order. This price includes postage and handling within the United States. Minnesota residents must add 6.5% sales tax. For additional quantities, please order in multiples of five. For Canadian and foreign orders, add postage and handling charges as above. Credit card (VISA, Master Card, American Express) orders are accepted. Charge card orders only may be phoned free ($15.00 minimum order) within the U.S.A. or Canada by dialing 1-800-THE-MOON. Customer service calls dial 1-612-291-1970. Mail orders to:

LLEWELLYN PUBLICATIONS
P.O. Box 64383, Dept. 667, St. Paul, MN 55164-383, U.S.A.

THE BOOK OF GODDESSES & HEROINES
by Patricia Monaghan
The Book of Goddesses & Heroines is a historical landmark, a must for everyone interested in Goddesses and Goddess worship. It is not an effort to trivialize the beliefs of matriarchal cultures. It is not a collection of Goddess descriptions penned by biased male historians throughout the ages. It is the complete, non-biased account of Goddesses of every cultural and geographic area, including African, Egyptian, Japanese, Korean, Persian, Australian, Pacific, Latin American, British, Irish, Scottish, Welsh, Chinese, Greek, Icelandic, Italian, Finnish, German, Scandinavian, Indian, Tibetan, Mesopotamian, North American, Semitic and Slavic Goddesses!

Unlike some of the male historians before her, Patricia Monaghan eliminates as much bias as possible from her Goddess stories. Envisioning herself as a woman who might have revered each of these Goddesses, she has done away with language that referred to the deities in relation to their male counterparts, as well as with culturally relative terms such as "married" or "fertility cult." The beliefs of the cultures and the attributes of the Goddesses have been left intact.

Plus, this book has a new, complete index. If you are more concerned about finding a Goddess of war than you are a Goddess of a given country, this index will lead you to the right page. This is especially useful for anyone seeking to do Goddess rituals. Your work will be twice as efficient and effective with this detailed and easy-to-use book.
0-87542-573-9, 456 pgs., 6 x 9, photos, softcover   **$17.95**

COMING INTO THE LIGHT: Rituals of Egyptian Magick
by Gerald & Betty Schueler
Coming into the Light is the name that the ancient Egyptians gave to a series of magickal texts known to us today as *The Book of the Dead.* *Coming into the Light* provides modern translations of these famous texts, and shows that they are not simply religious prayers or spells to be spoken over the body of a dead king, but rituals to be performed by living magicians who seek to know the truth about themselves and their world. Basic Egyptian philosophical and religious concepts are explained and explored, and ritual texts for a wide variety of magickal use are presented. For example, the Ritual of the Opening of the Mouth, perhaps the most well-known of Egyptian rituals, allows a magician to enter into the higher regions of the Magickal Universe without losing consciousness. Enough of this ancient wisdom has been passed down to us so that today we may gain a unique insight into the workings of those powerful magicians who performed their operations thousands of years ago.
0-87542-713-8, 378 pgs., 6 x 9, 24 color plates, softcover $14.95

THE GODDESS SEKHMET
Psychospiritual Exercises of the Fifth Way
by Robert Masters, Ph.D.
Here is the story of the ancient goddess Sekhmet, a form of the Great Mother related to the creative and destructive power of the Sun. Most importantly, this book presents Sekhmet as an archetypal force, guiding the reader into a positive direct experience of the Living Goddess, her teachings and life-transforming rituals.

As a result of Dr. Masters' direct encounter with Sekhmet in a series of telepathic trance states, he has received the teachings of the sacred books of Sekhmet that were lost, pillaged from the temples and destroyed by unbelievers. This is a book of the reconstructed scriptures and spiritual disciplines that will open its readers to the mysteries, supernatural powers, and mind-body-spirit transformations of Sekhmet. Half of *The Goddess Sekhmet* consists of Psychospiritual Exercises, which are techniques that can be practiced primarily as psychological exercises and as a way to improve the health and functioning of the brain and nervous system. By doing the exercises, the reader will increase the awareness of, and ability to use, more latent human potentials.
0-87542-485-6, 256 pgs., 6 x 9, photos, softcover   **$12.95**
0-87542-495-3, 256 pgs., 6 x 9, photos, hardcover   **$22.95**

THE GODDESS AND THE TREE: The Witches Qabala, Book I
(Formerly *The Witches' Qabala*)
by Ellen Cannon Reed
There is a tree that has its roots in heaven—a tree that contains all that is, and was, and will be. On it, are meditations that can, when properly applied, bring about specific spiritual experiences and solve spiritual problems. It bears on its branches a guide for spiritual growth. It bears the Goddess in all Her beauty, and the God in all His strengths. It contains a system for training the mind, making the proper astral contacts, guiding your own spiritual growth, or that of others, step by step. It contains a method for helping you and others experience the Mysteries.

This system, so long spurned by paganfolk, can serve all of them well, even with only the most basic knowledge of the subject. The author has brought the two schools together, showing how the religious aspect of the pagan paths maybe developed and served by the techniques inherent in the Qabala.
0-87542-666-2, 192 pgs., 5 1/4 x 8, illus., softcover   **$7.95**

THE TRUTH ABOUT EGYPTIAN MAGICK
by Gerald and Betty Schueler
Surveys the history, forms of Egyptian magick, the gods and goddesses, the sacred texts, High and Low Magick, *The Book of the Dead*, the use of ancient hieroglyphics, rituals, myths and the role of Egyptian magick today.
0-87542-735-9, 32 pgs., 5 1/2 x 8 1/2, softcover $2.00

THE WITCHES TAROT: The Witches Qabala, Book II
by Ellen Cannon Reed
In this book Ellen Cannon Reed has further defined the complex, inner workings of the Qabalistic Tree of Life. She brings together the Major and Minor Arcana cards with the Tree of Life to provide readers with a unique insight on the meaning of the Paths on the Tree. Included is a complete section on divination with the Tarot cards, with several layout patterns and explanations clearly presented.

The Major Arcana cards are also keys to Pathworking astral journeys through the Tree of Life. Reed explains Pathworking and gives several examples. An appendix gives a list of correspondences for each of the Paths including the associated Tarot card, Hebrew letter, colors, astrological attribution, animal, gem, and suggested meditation. This book is a valuable addition to the literature of the Tarot and the Qabala.
0-87542-668-9, 320 pgs., 5 1/4 x 8, illus., softcover $9.95

THE WITCHES TAROT DECK
by Ellen Cannon Reed and Martin Cannon
Author Ellen Cannon Reed has created the first Tarot deck specifically for Pagans and Wiccans. Reed, herself a Wiccan High Priestess, developed The Witches Tarot as a way to teach the truths of the Hebrew Kabbalah from a clear and distinctly Pagan point of view. Changes include a Horned One in place of the traditional Devil, a High Priest in place of the old Hierophant, and a Seeker in place of the Hermit. Comes complete with an instruction booklet that tells you what the cards mean and explains how to use the "Celtic Cross" and "Four Seasons" layouts. The gorgeous, detailed paintings by Martin Cannon make this a true combination of new beauty and ancient symbolism. Even many non-Pagans have reported excellent results with the cards and appreciate their colorful and timeless beauty.
0-87542-669-7, boxed set: 78 full-color cards with booklet $17.95

WICCA: A Guide for the Solitary Practitioner
by Scott Cunningham
Wicca is a book of life, and how to live magically, spiritually, and wholly attuned with Nature. It is a book of sense and common sense, not only about magic, but about religion and how to achieve a much needed and wholesome relationship with our Earth. Cunningham presents Wicca as it is today: a gentle, Earth-oriented religion dedicated to the Goddess and God.

Here is a positive, practical introduction to the religion of Wicca, designed so that any interested person can learn to practice the religion alone, anywhere in the world. It presents Wicca honestly and clearly, without the pseudo-history that permeates other books. It shows that Wicca is a vital, satisfying part of twentieth century life.

This book presents the theory and practice of Wicca from an individual's perspective. The section on the Standing Stones Book of Shadows contains solitary rituals for the Esbats and Sabbats. This book, based on the author's nearly two decades of Wiccan practice, presents an eclectic picture of various aspects of this religion. Exercises designed to develop magical proficiency, a self-dedication ritual, herb, crystal and rune magic, recipes for Sabbat feasts, are included in this excellent book.
0-87542-118-0, 240 pgs., 6 x 9, illus., softcover   **$9.95**

BUCKLAND'S COMPLETE BOOK OF WITCHCRAFT
by Raymond Buckland
Here is the most complete resource to the study and practice of modern, non-denominational Wicca. This is a self-study course for the solitary or group. Included are rituals; exercises for developing psychic talents; information on all major "sects" of the Craft; sections on tools, beliefs, dreams, meditations, divination, herbal lore, healing, ritual clothing and much, much more. This book unites theory and practice into a comprehensive course designed to help you develop into a practicing Witch. Workbook-type format, profusely illustrated and full of music and chants, it takes you from A to Z in the study of Witchcraft.

Never before has so much information on the Craft of the Wise been collected in one place. Traditionally, there are three degrees of advancement in most Wiccan traditions. When you have completed studying this book, you will be the equivalent of a Third-Degree Witch. Even those who have practiced Wicca for years find useful information in this book, and many covens are using this for their textbook. If you want to become a Witch, or if you merely want to find out what Witchcraft is really about, you will find no better book than this.
0-87542-050-8, 272 pgs., 8 1/2 x 11, illus., softcover   **$14.95**